EXALTAVIT HUMILES

The Imitation
of Mary

BY
THOMAS à KEMPIS

Extracts from the Original Works of
THOMAS à KEMPIS

Selected and Edited by
DR. ALBIN DE CIGALA

Foreword by SAM GUZMAN

Translated from
the French edition by
a Dominican Sister

Angelico Press

NIHIL OBSTAT
EDWARD A. CERNY, *SS., D.D.*
Censor Librorum

IMPRIMATUR:
MICHAEL J. CURLEY, *D.D.*
Archbishop of Baltimore and Washington

February 17, 1947

Angelico Press reprint edition, © 2020
First published 1948 by The Newman Press.

For information, address:
Angelico Press
169 Monitor St., Brooklyn, NY 11222
www.angelicopress.com

pb: 978-1-62138-528-8
hb: 978-1-62138-529-5

Cover Design: Michael Schrauzer

CONTENTS

FOREWORD

BY *Sam Guzman*

The mystery of the Church is inseparable from the mystery of Mary most holy. For every *sacramentum* of the Church is somehow related to the mystery of her presence and maternal love.

It was her *fiat* that was the hinge of history, undoing the curse and bringing about the central mystery of the Christian faith, the Incarnation of the God-Man, Jesus Christ. It was her command that brought about the first of his signs and wonders at Cana in Galilee. It was she who accompanied him on the painful way of the Cross, and she who co-redeemed humanity with him by the sword that rent her heart. It was she who was there in the cenacle on the day of Pentecost, calling forth the tongues of fire to descend on the apostles, the first manifestation of transfigured humanity.

And her presence continues with us, for she is present by her love in every sacrament—most of all in the Eucharist, for the body of Christ that we receive came entirely from her body, and their hearts are indeed so united as to beat as one. The soul of every Christian, St. Louis de Montfort tells us, is divinized in her spiritual womb. And she is there in the Apocalypse at the revelation of the consummation of all things, robed in the splendor of the stars of heaven. She is the zenith, the apex of creation's return to God, drawing all creation after her. There is no redemption, no salvation without her. It is no wonder, then, that the fathers of the Church cried out in wonder, "De Maria nunquam satis," of Mary there is never enough [said or sung]. Indeed, every saint throughout the centuries has sung in varying degrees the praises of the Mother of God.

But what of the great Thomas à Kempis?

While not formally sainted, few would question his holiness and deep devotion. After all, he is the author of one of the most beloved spiritual works of all time, *The Imitation of Christ.* Some have claimed, though it is difficult to prove, that this work is second only to the Bible itself in copies printed. In his time, he was known as a greater preacher, writer, and loving and devout soul, and his reputation has not dimmed through the centuries.

Yet, for all this, he does not mention the Blessed Virgin even once in this magnificent work. Did he not love her? Does he believe she is superfluous in the spiritual life? Some would argue so, making à Kempis out to be a sort of proto-Protestant evangelical who had little use for the distinctively Catholic (an argument made easier by the removal of the fourth book of the *Imitation*, on devotion to the Eucharist, by some publishers).

As the work you are about to read makes clear, however, nothing could be further from the truth. With a heart burning with love, he cries out: "O Mother, more beloved than all mothers, O Mary, if sometimes I have forgotten you, I regret and weep for it today.... Kneeling I salute you, I bow before you, I join my hands and prostrate myself, so that you may listen with greater love to my prayer."

No, à Kempis's heart was far from cold toward the Virgin Mary. It was rather radiant with love toward her. The work that follows is compiled from his many devotional writings about her. In its selections it is unique, preserving the poetic heart of its author better than other edited works published under the same name that attempted to do the same thing. It is a sort of psalter, a song book of praise, to the woman that made his heart sing—a truly worthy companion to *The Imitation of Christ*.

It is a rule proven by the facts of history that, where Marian devotion has flowered, there has been a flowering of Christian culture in architecture, music, theology, art, and above all in renewed devotion. The marks of Mary's presence are a love for the poor and downtrodden, the earth and all growing things, and humility and chastity in all their various forms, combined with the most exuberant acts of love incarnated in elements of glass and stone, pigment and canvas, word and song. In short, under the warmth of her maternal gaze the seed potential of human creativity unfolds in all its splendor, breaking forth in sunlike radiance.

We live in uncertain times in which all that makes us human is under increasing threat from a many-headed hydra of forces: mass media, corporate-driven consumerism, materialism, artificial intelligence, government intrusion, a broken education system, and far more. The Church, too, is reeling from scandals, a loss of the anchoring memory of tradition, and the dual forces of secularization and a vague and formless spirituality. Like Lazarus bound in the tomb, we are succumbing to forces of decay and degeneration.

If we are to see the revivification we so desperately need, we must rediscover the Mother, who longs to wrap us all in her life-giving embrace. The future of Christianity depends on this task. Sheltered under her mantle of light, Christianity will again flourish, though perhaps not statistically. It may indeed continue to shrink outwardly. But it will be accompanied by a deepening of the spirit, a renewal of the heart, and a creative outpouring akin to the fire of Pentecost that will set hearts ablaze and renew the face of the earth.

It is my hope that this small but potent work will be a seed planted in the hearts of those who read it, bearing fruit in due season. May it lead to a true renaissance of love, and may it lead many into the arms of the one "clothed with the sun, with the moon under her feet and a crown of twelve stars on her head" (Rev 12:1)—our compassionate Mother and the Mother of all creation.

EXTRACTS FROM THE
PREFACE TO THE FRENCH EDITION

The Imitation of Christ, the most beautiful of books coming from the hand of man, ought to have as a counterpart *The Imitation of Mary*. However, we do not have it in a completely finished form; we only possess it scattered throughout the works of Thomas à Kempis.

The century which brought forth *The Imitation of Christ*— the fifteenth—is the century which saw completed the greater part of the Gothic churches dedicated to the Virgin in France and the Low Countries, from Notre Dame of Paris to the Cathedral of Cologne.

This is the most flourishing epoch of the cult of the Virgin, the golden age of devotion to Mary. The name of Mary is found ever at the side of that of Jesus, as, for example, on the standard of Jeanne d'Arc.

Besides, we notice with sorrow that the author of *The Imitation of Christ* does not speak a single time of devotion to the Virgin Mary in this divine book which treats of all the subjects of Christian Mysticism.

Was it forgetfulness or negligence? Neither one nor the other.

Thomas à Kempis, canon of Cologne, and abbé of Mount St. Agnes whose church is dedicated to the Virgin, has written entire chapters on devotion to Mary in his divers works.

But the copyists who transcribed the first Books of *The Imitation*, finished by Kempis, thus leaving the fourth incomplete, did not know how to arrange the passages treating of the devotion to the Virgin Mary in the immense production of the author.

The present work, which is only the work of an analyst, we have undertaken. We have been able to extract from the different works of Kempis whole chapters on the devotion to Mary written in the same poetic and rhythmic language as is *The Imitation*. Everything seems to indicate that they were destined to form a Fifth Book of the Treatise on the Interior Life, following that of the Eucharist. One finds in it the same doctrine of elevated theology and the same grace of poetry in its forms. . .

We have arranged this work according to the mysteries of the life of Mary; joyous mysteries, sorrowful mysteries, glorious mysteries.

The reading of it will thus be easier. It is especially fitting to recall the advice of the author: "You must read not only with the mind, but above all with the heart."

We have tried to enclose our heart in that of our Mother. Likewise may you do, all you who shall read this book!

Dr. Albin de Cigala
Faculty of Paris
Doctor of Theology and Philosophy

The homilies and meditations are the work of Dr. de Cigala who comments on the extract of Kempis in order to aid the reader to derive more fully its fruits.

SOLILOQUIES OF THE SOUL

—Thomas à Kempis

Read, O my son, or rather chant while reading,
These sweet versicles in honor of Mary.
Take them as a viaticum for the soul;
Take them as one does a staff for a journey.
Read often, and re-read with devotion while praying.

May Jesus and Mary be for you in life,
At all times, in every place, your sole company,
For fear that you may wander alone or unguided,
Shedding without the perfumes from within.

You will find here a treatise on Mary, brief,
But a treatise full of sweetness for meditation,
And a treatise full of strength to protect you well.

Meditate on it often, and often pray, too,
Saying with a full heart: Hail, Mary.

PART ONE

THE JOYFUL MYSTERIES

CHAPTER I

THE IMITATION OF
THE BLESSED VIRGIN MARY

I.

Many young girls, says the author of Wisdom, have amassed riches, but you, O Mary, you surpass them all greatly.

Children, be faithful imitators of Jesus, and perfect imitators of Mary.

It matters a great deal, it matters for your salvation, for the honor of Jesus and the glory of Mary, that you always be devout in your prayers, sober in your words, discreet in your looks.

In brief, be scrupulously disciplined in all your deeds.

II.

Do you wish to praise Mary worthily; do you wish to praise her in all magnificence?

Be simple, like the simple children of God, without deception, without envy, without criticism, without murmuring, and without any suspicion.

Support all adverse things with charity, with great patience and great humility.

For Jesus, for Mary, and in order to imitate the saints, watch here below, watch and be yourselves saints.

To one who knows how to offer his life to the Divine Trinity, all that is bitter here on earth appears sweet, and all that seems heavy appears very light.

Such is the fruit of the remembrance of Mary and Jesus.

1

III. Prayer:

O Mary, O sweet Mother of my Jesus, I beg you, deign to open
to your poor servant both your maternal compassion and your
love, laden with sweetness.

Pour into my heart one drop of your tenderness so that I may
love you with a pure heart, you, O Mother, the sweetest of all
mothers, so that I may imitate you and Jesus.

> Listen to me, Mother, listen to me, Mary,
> kneeling I salute you: Ave Maria.
> The sky rejoices and the earth smiles
> when the heart says: Ave Maria.
> Satan flies afar and all hell shudders
> when the heart says: Ave Maria.
> The world seems small and the flesh trembles
> when the heart says: Ave Maria.
> Sadness flees and happiness reigns
> when the heart says: Ave Maria.
> Lukewarmness disappears and love reappears
> when the heart says: Ave Maria.
> Devotion grows and compunction is born
> when the heart says: Ave Maria.
> Hope gushes forth and consolation increases
> when the heart says: Ave Maria.
> The whole soul rekindles and love grows tender
> when the heart says: Ave Maria.

So rich and so great is the sweetness of this prayer, that it
could not be expressed in words.

Thus, again I kneel before you, O Mary, O Virgin, O Mother
filled with goodness, and I say to you, over and over, with
reverence and devotion:

Hail, Mary, Hail! Receive this pious salutation, and with it receive me, O Mother, within your bosom.

(Discourse XXV)

HOMILY

THE MODEL AND IMITATION

I. To imitate is to reproduce a model: but the model can be larger or smaller than the reproduction. Thus it is in the imitation of Jesus, of Mary and of the Saints. The models in this case are greater than nature. We can, nevertheless, succeed in resembling them by reproducing their life.

II. Life is a complexity of virtues and of faults, of forces and of instincts. Nothing is evil by nature, but according as one rises or falls, one becomes good or bad. It can be said that a middle way does not exist. One must choose vice or virtue. To practice virtue an effort must be made; such is the meaning of the Latin word: *virtus*. To follow vice it suffices to let oneself go; such is the meaning of the Latin word: *vitium*.

III. The Christian soul, in the face of the divine model, Mary, exalts itself to the practice of the virtues which it admires in her who is, at the same time, a sublime model and an admirable mistress, an example and a mother.

MEDITATION

THE WORK OF SANCTIFICATION

It is a science to know how to regard a model; it is an art to be able to reproduce it. This art and this work contain the whole secret of the spiritual life. Consideration is meditation or contemplation, the study of divine harmonies. We emulate the Saints, and in order to do so we must suffer. That is why grief teaches more than joy. He who has not suffered, what does he know? A heart which loves has already been half-opened by a sword. Strike the heart, for in it is genius, said the poet; and there also is sanctity.

Practice: To wear a medal of Mary, as beautiful as possible, is an easy means of recalling that to imitate her one must make an effort.

Thought: To one who loves Mary everything seems sweet and light. *Amara dulcia fiunt, gravia levia veniunt.*

CHAPTER II

DUTIES TOWARD MARY

I.

Choose, O my son, before all things, Mary for mother, for advocate, and for model. Greet her every day with the Angelic Salutation. This salutation pleases her above all others.

If sometimes the devil tempts you and turns you from your duties as a devout servant of Mary, do not permit that to stop you from invoking her always. Think always of Mary; repeat over and over the name of Mary. Honor Mary; glorify Mary in everything; prostrate yourself before Mary; give yourself again to Mary.

Live with Mary; meditate with Mary; rejoice with Mary; weep with Mary; work with Mary; watch with Mary; act with Mary; rest with Mary.

With Mary, bear Jesus in your arms; live at Nazareth with Mary.

Go to Jerusalem, go with Mary; search, as Mary did, for Jesus.

Remain near the cross with Mary, weep for Jesus; weep for Him with Mary; with Mary bury Jesus in the tomb; rise with Jesus and with Mary.

Rise to heaven with Jesus and with Mary. Live always with Mary in life and in death.

II.

If you know how to think and act in this way, you will advance rapidly in perfection. Mary will protect you with all her power, and Jesus will hear you in His gentle mercy.

What we do is very little. It is nothing. Nevertheless, if we do it with Mary, we shall rise little by little to God our Father. We shall always find near Him consolation and joy.

Happy is he who knows how to keep always near him Jesus and Mary as hosts of his table, consolers in his troubles, help in his danger, counsel in his doubt, protectors at his death.

Happy is he who considering himself in this world as a wayfarer, and as a stranger, keeps Jesus for a companion and Mary for a hostess.

III. Prayer:

O Mother, I come to you filled with hope. I come to you recalling the exultant joy which the Archangel Gabriel once brought
to you when, falling on his knees before you, he saluted your
virginity, saying respectfully: Hail, Mary, the Lord is with
thee.

This greeting I say to you again, O Mother, with the heart,
and, if I could, with the voice of all the faithful, so that thus
all creatures may sing with me from the depth of their souls
and their being:

> Ave Maria, full of grace, the Lord is with thee, thou
> art blessed, O Mother, among all women, and Jesus the
> fruit of thy womb, is blessed on earth and in heaven,
> today and always.

(Soliloquy of the Soul, Chap. XVIII)

HOMILY
The Titles and Functions of Mary

I. Our duties toward Mary flow from the titles and functions of Mary herself. Her titles are the most beautiful and the most sweet: first, that of mother, which one says lovingly at any age; next, the title of model, which one considers with admiration and joy.

II. Her functions are in relation to her titles: the names given by God are at once an evocation and a creation of the qualities signified by the names and titles themselves. Thus Mary, in virtue of her titles, exercises her functions of mother who consoles, supports and nourishes, of advocate who counsels, directs and defends, and lastly of model who exalts and attracts.

III. In a prayer exultant with joy and full of love, the faithful beg Mary to teach them to pray as the angels pray. Prayer, here on earth, cries, weeps or is silent; prayer, in heaven, is a vision, a contemplation and an ecstasy.

MEDITATION
The Supernatural Life

To live is to rise, it is to rise above the earth: see the flowers which live and those which are dead. Man loves to live so fully that he wishes to live a double life: hence arises love, which is the most beautiful thing on the earth.

This earthly existence is not, however, all of life. There is the life of the soul, without which love itself is nothing. Love which seems not to be immortal does not satisfy the heart. The life which does not die is the supernatural life, the life of grace.

Mary has been given to us for a model and for a mother in this new life added to the earthly life. He who has not known this desire to rise still higher, has not as yet lived. Let us live, then, not in order to die, but in order to attain immortality.

Practice: Reciting the Rosary, or simply carrying it, is a practice which aids the soul to rise to heavenly thoughts.

Thought: To live with Mary is to live in the security and the happiness of heaven.
Bene et secure ambulat qui Mariam in corde portat.

CHAPTER III

VIRTUES AND TASKS OF
A GOOD SERVANT OF MARY

I.

Do you always wish to do what is pleasing to Mary?

Be humble, patient, chaste, reserved in everything, full of mildness, an interior man, filled with zeal, little versed in exterior matters, recollected.

Read often, write often, but most often pray.

The service of Mary should seem to you neither long nor laborious, but on the contrary always delightful, always full of happiness, always eager.

To serve with your heart and mind such a mistress is always a work pious and useful for salvation.

The most lowly offerings are acceptable to her as equivalent to the most solemn, when they are proffered with love, with spontaneity, and with devotion.

She knows how little we are able to give, and she requires not the impossible from her children.

A merciful sovereign and queen of mildness, she is above all a mother. As a mother, she knows only how to compassionate with the little and the poor, she who has given to the world mercy in Jesus.

II.

Learn then to call upon Jesus in everything, and you will be aided both in perils of the soul and of the body.

Have Jesus always in your heart, in happiness, and you will never be overcome by human distress.

Say often the Hail Mary: you will find in it joy and peace: no prayer is more beautiful than the Our Father; none is sweeter and gentler than the Hail Mary.

Pray as the angel prayed before Mary: work as a faithful servant works, and you shall have in heaven your crown and place.

He who knows how to nourish his soul with prayer, he who
knows how to pray with the sacred texts, will never know
aridity in devotion.

Strive thus constantly to honor the names of Jesus and Mary in
your heart and with your lips.

III.

Wherever you may go, or wherever you may be, implore Jesus
and call upon Mary.

Have as a rule of life and as a help in time of need this pious
invocation: Guide, O my Lord, always guide my way in Thy
presence.

He who in his heart bears Jesus and Mary always works well,
always conducts himself well.

Sing these two names, sing them in your heart, sing them with
your lips, sing them with your hands.

Let your looks seek them, let your eyes implore them, let your
arms embrace them, let your knees adore them.

IV. Prayer:

O Mary, O Mother full of mercy, receive close to you, your servant wandering without consolation, in the midst of his trials.

Look, O my Queen, look at my affliction and open to me your
heart full of consolation.

Here I am praying and saying in my distress, that I shall not
cease nor leave you until you have had pity on me.

I know, O Mother, your incomparable sweetness, I know the
maternal flame of your noble heart, I know the fullness of
love that fills it, and that I may have full hope in you.

Also, I take refuge with you, O my Mother, so that in joy as in
sorrow, I may receive your watchful succor and listen to your
maternal consolation.

(The Valley of Lilies, Chap. XIII)

HOMILY

The Virtues that a Good Servant of Mary Ought to Practice and the Offices He Ought to Fulfill

I.   The Latins have two words to designate the good actions to be accomplished in life. The word *virtus* in order to designate an action made with effort and good will, and the word *officium* in order to characterize an action accomplished as a duty but without attachment of the heart. That which is required here of a good servant of Mary are virtues, that is to say, meritorious acts, élans of the heart and not only works which domestics themselves can fulfill. There are firstly the interior virtues: humility, patience and purity.

II.   Afterwards there are the exterior virtues or virtues of action: effort in work, elevation of the mind, union in mental prayer, zeal in vocal prayer.

III.   These united virtues ought to animate all practices of devotion, if we wish that these practices be spiritual acts of meritorious virtue and not only material offices of remunerated work. Thus Mary acted; thus we ourselves should act.

IV.   The servant therefore asks of Mary, who is a mother and a model, to aid him in this work and to console him amid the difficulties of the work.

MEDITATION

The Active Life

Life is like fire: it only preserves itself while communicating itself. The ancients used to represent it by a flame and that is, indeed, the truth. To live it is necessary to act. The active life supposes will and effort. Mary has known and practiced this life, as all the Saints have practiced it.

Life which passes selfishly, disillusions and engenders boredom; *taedium vitae*. Unfortunate is the soul which permits itself to live without rising! He will have lived most who will have acted most, through his heart, through his soul and through his body, through love, through the mind and through works.

Is there a more beautiful model than Mary, in the Temple, at Nazareth, on Calvary, with St. John? Such a one has lived long, who has lived little, said a wise man. Let us live like Mary and with Mary.

Practice: Do not allow a single day to pass without having made an effort in at least one small thing.

Thought: A lukewarm life is a dull one; live as Mary did.
Aspice Mariam, contemplare et mirare.

CHAPTER IV

GRANDEURS AND GLORIES OF MARY

I.

Who is she who rises from the emptiness of this world steeped in the delights of Paradise?

O Mary, greater than the heavens, you have the world under your feet, and you are seated close to God, on the throne of honor which Jesus gave you.

Your mercy which surpasses all mercy draws me to you, for you are ever the aid and consolation of those who suffer.

I have need, O Mother, of being consoled and fortified. More than that, I have need of the grace of your Son because I know that without it I can accomplish nothing.

You are able, O my Mother, if you wish, to lift me up and help me with your powerful succor. You can comfort me with your abundant consolation.

I feel myself engulfed by temptation, so I run to you, since I feel that near you I shall find help as well as pity.

II.

And if I may approach your majesty and greet you with reverence and honor, I feel that I must approach you with love.

There is no praise which I can offer you; rather, I am forced to present to you supplication.

He who wishes to come near you irreverently, will be confounded: therefore I wish to come to you, O Mother, with confidence, with respect, with humility, so as to merit your clemency and your help.

Yes, it is with respect, with love and confidence that I come, O Mary, to offer you in my turn the salutation the angel offered you kneeling.

I offer it to you, arms extended and hands upraised, I offer it to you thousands and thousands of times and I beg every one to offer it for me, because I know of nothing sweeter that I may give.

11

III. Prayer:

O Mother, more beloved than all mothers, O Mary, if sometimes I have forgotten you, I regret and weep for it today.

But you, oh! do not forget me, you who alone brought forth mercy by giving birth to Jesus.

Kneeling, I salute you, I bow before you, I join my hands and prostrate myself, so that you may listen with greater love to my prayer.

I say before you, and I wish ever to repeat it:

> "Hail Mary, full of grace the Lord is with you;
> you are blessed among all women, and Jesus,
> the fruit of your womb, is blessed."

(Soliloquy of the Soul, Chap. XXIII)

HOMILY

THE EMINENT DIGNITY OF THE MOTHER OF GOD

I. The dignity of a person or of a being is measured by its function. There is not on earth, nor even in heaven, a function equal to that of the divine maternity of Mary. Mary is truly *Theotókos,* Mother of God and at the same time Mother of the Savior, because in Jesus the divinity and the humanity are substantially united. There is therefore no dignity superior to the dignity of Mary.

II. This eminent maternal dignity confers on Mary divine prerogatives at the same time that it infuses into her human tenderness superior to the most exquisite tenderness of mothers on earth. Even from the view point of the physical function, of the beauty of the woman and of the mother, Mary is above all those who have been outstanding in the world by their charms and attractions. St. Dennis, the Areopagite, refined Athenian and disciple of St. Paul, having gone to Jerusalem and having seen Mary, found her so beautiful that he wished to prostrate himself before her as before a goddess. Thus should we do in spirit.

III. It is what the disciple promises enthusiastically in the prayer addressed to Mary.

MEDITATION

THE USE OF TIME

Between the past which escapes us and the future which does not belong to us, there is the present which alone we possess. This is the time of action and of duty. To employ the present well is to enrich your life; to waste it is to die with it.

The first rule to use time well, is to use it and not to lose it. Next, to use it in time and not to act at random. Finally, to use it profitably and not without goal and rule; put off nothing, delay nothing until later. This is the secret, par excellence, of success.

Mary, here again, can serve us as model. She was undoubted-
ly the valiant and diligent woman of whom the Gospel speaks.
She fulfilled with perfection the motto of the noble Romans:
Domi mansit, lanam fecit. Mary, indeed, was at once Israelite by
birth and Roman by adoption. She is the perfect type of woman
in the double sense of: *femina et mulier.* Let us reproduce this
model and this type.

Practice: St. Francis of Sales purchased by an alms each hour
            which he thought to have lost or misused: imitate
            him.

Thought: The thought of Mary is a consolation and a protec-
            tion: *Solamen et dictamen.*

Chapter V

OUR DUTIES TO MARY

I.

You must still learn, my son, how to seek God as Mary did.

You must lean upon her powerful help, and be ever doubtful of your own strength, for fear of being enmeshed here below in your passions.

Everyday you should rise above yourself with new thoughts, and tender your desires to heaven, toward the heaven in which you see Mary your Queen, near Jesus the King, and in the midst of the court of angels.

Alas! Often our weakness will force us to descend into this valley of tears!

It is then above all that it will be necessary to make an effort to raise the voice in frequent supplication to Mary, who is the mother of mercy, so that she may tell her merciful Son how our soul lacks the wine of fervor, how it has need of the perfume of piety in order to be able to praise Him as one should praise God.

Because He alone, in truth, hastens to succor those who in order to please Him have scorned the world, and those who are for His sake scorned by the world, because of His Name and His holy Gospel.

II.

It is often important, indeed, to know of a refuge in which one may hide oneself against storms, in the presence of tempests of tribulation.

There is no spot, no place more secure, no port more tranquil than the bosom of Mary.

So there is no runner more rapid to support us against the blows of the enemy, than an ardent prayer, rising from the plain to the well-armed stronghold of the Virgin Mary. This stronghold is the same one in which Jesus entered to be clothed therein with a body like unto an armor, so as to chase afar the prince of darkness.

15

Enter you, too, within that fortress so as to be sheltered from those who assail you.

Remain under the mantle of the Virgin Mary; you will be protected by the arms of a mother.

The prayer of Mary puts to flight the destructive rabble of evil enemies: her aid snatches us from imminent peril.

Near her, he who wavers finds support, and he who is abandoned, help.

It is a boon, a very great boon, for you, if you know how to show yourself worthy in this regard, and at the same time strive attentively to please the Virgin Mary in everything.

You will thus merit her graces here below, and His glory on high in the company of the saints.

Attach yourself to her, and do not leave her until she has granted you her blessing so as to lead you to heaven.

III. Prayer:

O Mary, O mistress filled with clemency, in the name of pure love and affection, I remain at your feet. Give to my heart, I beg you, an increase of confidence.

Fear pursues me and doubt gnaws at me; despair assails me in the midst of temptations: only one thing is still able to console me: it is that I have sought to be heard by you. O Mother, I entrust myself to your heart.

(Monastic Enchiridion, Chap. IV)

HOMILY

Duty

I. Duty is a harsh word when it designates the obligation which binds a man to his post. It becomes a word full of sweetness when it is applied to the voluntary attentions which the heart suggests for a loved one. Our duties to Mary should be of this type. These duties, extremely pleasing, are those of a son to his mother, of a friend to his friend. The thought of heaven is a force, as the thought of love is an allurement. To raise one's thoughts is to raise oneself completely: *Altius cogita*.

II. It is in the life of the soul as in the present life; to think well is the beginning of doing well. To have great thoughts is to prepare for great actions. Mary's example in this case is more than a demonstration, it is an attraction and a help. Mary, says the Gospel, kept all these things in her heart. As Pascal said, great thoughts come from the heart; it is they that create the action. Too often has mysticism been reproached as being only a dream. The mysticism of the *Imitation* is an action, for it is perfection.

III. This action is arduous and often discouraging; besides, the soul begs Mary for confidence to be able to attain the goal of the spiritual life, which is heaven.

MEDITATION

The Beauties of Mary

The dream of every soul would be to see Mary in her heavenly splendor: Dante had this dream and tried to translate it into his *Paradise*. He represents Mary to us under the symbol of an aureole of pure gold and he refers to her only by the names of flowers: "blooming rose", "lily full of whiteness", "perfumed stem", "fragrant tree", "singing lyre", "sparkling sapphire", "soaring flame", "arc which rises". He sees her only in the midst of flowers, surrounded by stars, crowned with splendors. She epitomizes for him all which is charming here below in the being of a young girl, a virgin. The grace which extends itself in reflections, the beauty which radiates in magnificence, the love which gushes forth in transport.

Before this dazzlement the poet lowers his eyes and kneels with arms extended. So, it seems, we too should do in order to contemplate the beauties of Mary.

"Now raise thy view", St. Bernard then says to him, "unto the visage most resembling Christ: for, in her splendor only, shalt thou win the power to look on Him."

Mary, indeed, is beautiful, as all souls are beautiful by the reflection of Christ in them.

Practice: Imitate the saints who used to wear the shield and insignia of Mary, like the scapular and the rosary.

Thought: The remembrance of Mary is an aid and a support: *Adjuvat et sublevat.*

CHAPTER VI

OF THE POWER AND ABILITIES OF MARY

I.

Mary is faithful in her promises and generous in her gifts to her pious servants.

She enjoys the veneration of angels, but yet she accepts the attentions of men.

She tenderly sheds tears with the unhappy;
  she is compassionate with the sorrows of those who suffer;
  she comes to give help in the struggles of those who are tempted;
  she turns herself ever to those who pray to her.

All those who go with confidence and devotion to seek refuge with her and call upon her name find in her abundance and consolation.

A queen, she commands the angels in heaven and can send them to succor the needy.

In the same way, she has empire everywhere over the demons and can prevent them from harming her servants.

The demons dread the Queen of Heaven and her name alone suffices to disperse them.

They tremble before the awesome and holy name of Mary, before the name which causes joy to Christians, they no longer dare to show themselves before us or to try again their insidious assaults.

As soon as they hear this holy name resound, they tremble, they prostrate, they flee as before a burst of thunder from the sky.

And the more often this name is pronounced by us, the more it is invoked devotedly and piously, the more quickly the demons fly from us.

II.

It is for us a duty sacred above all, that of loving at every moment the holy name of Mary.

It ought to be for all the faithful, a cult;
  for Religious, a meditation;

for people in the world, a devotion;
for preachers, a veneration;
for those who suffer, a consolation;
in all dangers, a protection.
Mary is, truly, very near to God:
very dear to His Beloved Son, Jesus:
all powerful in her intercession in obtaining pardon and
succour for the unfortunate sons of Adam.
In all the circumstances of life, she intervenes with her Son
to obtain mercy for the culpable.
She, too, like Jesus Himself, is always heard, because of the
honor which is due to her.

Thus, therefore, let every pious Christian hurry to seek refuge
near Mary, if he wishes to escape from the shipwrecks of the
world, and to arrive at the port of eternal salvation.
We may indeed expect much from her, because although placed
above us all she loves to come to the least of us, happy to be
called advocate of the unfortunate, and more happy still,
mother of orphans.

III. Prayer:

O Mary, gentle Mother, beloved Mother above all,
you are the star on the horizon of the sea,
the star which smiles on the lost mariner,
the star which leads to the haven of peace.
Let it rise to you, O Mary, my simple prayer.
May the flame of my desire arise toward you, my cherished
Queen. Defend my cause at the tribunal of your Son, for no
one is found innocent before Him.

(Sermon to the Novices, Chap. XXIII)

HOMILY

THE PROTECTION OF MARY

Dominion and power are interesting in the hands of a protector only if he exercises them in favor of the protected.

I. The intervention of Mary for us, poor sinners, is necessary in every state of life. But especially in the moment of temptations; then above all is her protection useful to us. Temptations do not come to us from without, they originate within us still more than around us.

II. What are they? Each one knows them and recognizes them. Therefore let us seek Mary at the moment of these intimate struggles, in order to beg help of her and in order to receive consolation in them. *Solamen et dictamen.*

III. The faithful ask the Mother for the light to recognize their way and to be able to follow it well. Let us go to Mary, as to a mother and as to a queen.

MEDITATION

THE ROLE OF THE MOTHER IN MARY

That which denotes the grandeur and the charm of maternity in a woman are grief and tenderness. Grief which rends the heart as it rends the body in order to give life. Tenderness which binds the child to the mother and the mother to the child in such a way as to form only one being, as they form only one flesh.

All these characteristics are found physically in the human maternity of Mary, in her relations with Jesus, and mystically in the spiritual maternity of Mary vis-a-vis all Christians but more especially Religious.

The poem of maternal love which each mother lives, often without knowing it, is found in Mary with more grandeur and glory. It is necessary to know how to understand it and to meditate on it in order to feel it better and transfer it into life; this is the end of meditation.

Practice: Offer a sacrifice each day to Mary; however small it may be.

Thought: A mother is, in life, the bark and the star:
Stella et nacella.

CHAPTER VII

THE GREATNESS AND PRIVILEGES
OF MARY

I.

In order to succeed in knowing, at least in part, the greatness and dignity of the Virgin Mary, note briefly the eminent graces with which God has clothed her, while exalting her above angels and saints in heaven and above all men on earth.

She is the holy virgin, she is the beloved mother, of whom is said in the Church and throughout the universe, "You are raised, Holy Mother of God, higher than the angels, raised to the throne of Heaven."

Review with care the deeds and acts of the ancient patriarchs. It is from their root that Mary was born, virgin and mother equally, a rose without thorns amid the thickets.

Just as formerly Christ was prefigured in His birth, in His death, and in His life,

> by patriarchs, prophets, and kings,
> by judges, priests, and levites,
> by doctors and finally by scribes,
> in words, in symbols and in signs:

Likewise, as by a divine ordination,

> the Blessed Virgin Mary was equally announced,
> by celebrated virgins of past epochs,
> by illustrious mothers,
> by exemplary widows,
> by all women living in sanctity.

II.

By testimony of the Holy Scripture Mary was from all time, and will be always,

> the holiest virgin among all virgins,
> the most beautiful woman among all women,
> the sweetest mother among all mothers,

23

the purest daughter among all daughters,
the gentlest mistress among all mistresses,
the most illustrious queen among all queens.
In her are found again assembled, dwelling and shining with
an unequalled brilliance,
all virginal beauty and all virtuous charm,
all divine thought and all the love of the heart,
every virtuous work and every fruit of sanctity.

Mary never had a predecessor,
she has not today an equal,
she will never have henceforth a peer.
Just as formerly among the holy temples that of Solomon was
the most adorned, the richest, the most renowned, the unique,
so, the symbolic temple of Mary surpasses in excellence the
temples of the saints. It alone merits more of love and glory.

III. Prayer:

O Mary, Star that shines in the sky, Virgin, Queen of Heaven,
Sovereign of the World, no woman can be compared with you,
no matter with whatever virtues heaven may have adorned
her, because you are unique in the midst of the elect.
God the Father sees you as you were before all ages, and created
you upon earth, at the selected time, in order to make of
you the Mother of His Son.
O Miracle ineffable, O joy unhoped for! This Son of the Living
God to save the universe becomes your Son, and you are
His mother!
Thus you become our mediatrix, and the mediatrix of the entire
world.
O Mary, the most beautiful of all women, let the whole world
glorify you, honor you, sing to you, and love you!
May every creature repeat your praises in heaven and on earth,
now and forever.

(Sermons to the Novices, XXV)

HOMILY

THE EMINENT DIGNITY OF THE MOTHER OF GOD

I. In the suggestive language of poetry, when we compare God to the sun, we liken Mary to the moon, as the planet which comes immediately after the greatest.

Thus it is in reality: Mary is, after God, the most beautiful and the greatest marvel of the universe. The dignity and the grandeur of a being is due to its functions.

What grandeur more sublime, what dignity more striking than those of "Mother of God"? The Greeks had created purposefully in order to designate it, a word, which applies only to Mary: *Theotókos,* "she who has brought forth God."

II. In the enumeration of the privileges of Mary, the beauty, the sweetness, the power, the force, and the majesty, nothing equal is found here on earth. Just as the Temple of Solomon was unique in the world, thus Mary is unique in the order of creation. But if grandeur frightens ordinarily, here it attracts, for to the grandeur is attached tenderness: the tenderness of a mother.

III. Hence the author asks Mary, in the final prayer, for the help of her power and the protection of her love: *Tutamen et solomen.*

MEDITATION

GRANDEURS AND TENDERNESS OF MARY

The enumeration of the privileges of Mary is her most beautiful eulogy, says St. Germain. You are, O my Mother, the panegyric of all the ages and of all spheres. You are great and you are powerful, you are sovereign and you are mistress, you are queen and you are woman, you are she who is always named, and you are she who cannot be named at her worth. You are the mother and you are the ineffable.

Your tenderness is that of a virginal heart, inserted in the flesh of a mother. Just as the mother gives us both of her soul and of her body in forming us within her womb, thus you give us of your heart and of your substance when we receive Jesus, your Son, in the Eucharist.

O inaccessible grandeur, O ineffable tenderness!

Practice: Recite often the litanies of the Holy Virgin which are a summary of her privileges.

Thought: O Mary, you surpass in greatness and sweetness all creatures: *Tu supergressa es universas, O Maria!*

Chapter VIII

ON THE BEAUTY AND LINEAGE OF MARY

I.

O Mary, illustrious Virgin,
    engendered from the fruitful race of patriarchs,
    nourished by the holy descendants of priests,
    O Mary, honored with the dignity of pontiffs,
    announced by the choir of prophets,
    heiress of the grandeur of kings,
    illustrious daughter of the house of David,
    supreme glory of the tribe of Juda.
Sacred heroine of the valiant people of Israel,
    living symbol of a holy nation,
    miraculous child of blessed parents,
    you merit glory and praise,
    you merit tenderness and love.

You are a treasure among all women,
    You, who even before the beginning of time
    had been chosen as the Mother of God.
The patriarchs desired your birth, O Mary,
    the wise prophets announced you,
    the just men and the kings bore witness to you,
    the people of Israel sighed for you,
    until the day when at last you appeared,
    O Mary, for the salvation of this dying world.

II.

Your name is proclaimed in the whole universe,
    O Mary! from the rising to the setting of the sun,
    Among all nations, Jews and Gentiles,
    Greeks and Latins, Romans and Scythians,
    Everywhere your name is announced with the Gospel.
Everywhere, too, and everyday your name is preached
    in churches and chapels,
    in cloisters, in fields, in deserts.

It is repeated by the little and the great,
    by priests and doctors and preachers,
    who all equally seek to praise you.
Yes, O Mary, together the choir of the just
    unites its harmonies and its voices,
    in order to chant your attractions,
    your grace and your holiness.
Its love is so great, its love is so gentle,
    that it can without ever tiring, chant,
    contemplate, meditate and fête your mysteries,
    Mindful of the words of Wisdom:
Those who eat of me yet hunger for this bread,
    those who drink of me still thirst for this wine.

III. Prayer:

Come then, O Mary, sweet Virgin whom I love!
Come then, my hope and my consolation!
Come, for when I am near you, when I hear your voice,
    it seems that I already possess all good,
    it seems that I am sheltered from all evil,
Recalling your sweet clemency,
    I come to seek refuge under your aegis,
    O Mary, you who know how to give
    to the weak, strength,
    to the captive, freedom,
    be for me all merciful,
    be by your love a mother to me.
Thus I shall know through having experienced it
    how you console with charm,
    and how you defend with assurance,
    all those who are faithful in serving you.

        (Soliloquy of the Soul, Chap. V)

HOMILY

The Splendor of the Race in Mary

I. Perfect beauty bears a new name; it is splendor. Splendor is itself a virtue. All virtue has, in effect, an active side and a passive side. It produces works which we see and it is produced by causes which we do not see. In Mary, the splendor and the illustriousness of her race operate these marvels which cause love and admiration to be born, which entice hearts and elevate souls. Let us be drawn to Mary: *Trahimur ad te,* chants the Liturgy.

II. This splendor in Mary arises from her race and her descent. She is the heir of a royal line which goes back to Joachim, to Solomon, to David, to Jesse, to Abraham, to Adam. Flowered stem, blessed branch which was to bear the divine fruit of the Eucharist: *Caro Christi, caro Mariae,* said St. Augustine.

III. Also, let us ask Mary, with the pious author of the *Imitation,* for the hope which is a source of consolation, awaiting the realization of love in heaven where we shall see our Mother and our Queen in all her splendor.

MEDITATION

Feminine Beauty

Beauty is not only a brilliance, it is also a harmony of the proportions which constitutes perfection. The man who would possess this harmony would be the perfect man. But there is in the beauty of a woman a more luminous and a more delicate grace which constitutes charm. Let her be queen or shepherdess, a great lady or a simple worker, a woman can always refine herself more than a man and arrive at this harmonious beauty of gestures if not of forms, which will make her particular charm.

Do not doubt that this be a virtue instead of coquetry, if it is used in the service of the good and in the perfection of the soul. All that requires effort, and an effort is always an act of virtue. Be careful, then, as St. Francis de Sales said, of your appearance and cultivate your heart, so that the fire which leaps forth from this heart, illumines your face with heavenly splendor equal to that of our divine mother Mary, the most beautiful of all women.

Practice: To make an effort every day to be gracious to everyone.

Thought: You are all beautiful, O Mary: *Tota pulchra es Maria.*

CHAPTER IX

SYMBOLS OF MARY

I.

Honor, praise and glory to God on high, who gives to you,
    O Mary, a grace greater than that of all the women in this
    world,
    and who gives to you in the other world a place of glory,
    near His throne in the highest heaven above all the choirs
    of angels and saints.

O glorious and admirable Virgin Mary,
    Mother, as well as Daughter, of your God,
    you merit all honor and glory.
You are the most great in your humility,
    the most beautiful in your virginity,
    the most ardent in your love,
    the most resigned in your patience.
You are the most gentle in your mercy,
    the most inflamed in your prayer,
    the most profound in your meditation,
    the most elevated in your contemplation,
    the most sensitive in your compassion,
    the most enlightened in your counsel,
    the most powerful in your help.

II.

You are, O Mary, the dwelling place of God,
    you are also, O Mary, the gate of heaven,
    the garden of delights, the source of graces,
    the glory of angels, the salvation of men.
You are the art of living, the splendor of virtue,
    the light of day, the hope of the unhappy,
    the health of the sick, the mother of orphans.
O Virgin of virgins, all beautiful and fragrant,
    you have in yourself, O Mary,
    the brilliance of the star, the charm of the rose,

the beauty of the dawn, the gentleness of the moon,
the depth of the pearl, the splendor of the sun.

III.

And in you too, O Virgin, so gentle,
  pure in your life, like to a lamb,
  simple in your heart, like a dove,
  prudent in the fashion of a noble mistress,
  submissive in the manner of a humble servant.

O Mary, holy tree, lofty and sublime cedar,
  vine heavy with grapes, fig tree covered with fruit,
  cypress tall and strong, palm tree full of glory,
  in you are found gathered all good things,
  through you are promised to us all delights.

We all hasten then to you, O Mary, as sons to a beloved mother,
as orphans to a mother whom they love.

Through your merits protect us from all evil. Through your
prayers deliver us from all peril.

IV. Prayer:

O Mary, golden rose, sweet and beautiful at once, may my
urgent prayers rise to you!

Here I stand, knocking at the door of your dwelling, assured
of obtaining your mercy, in the midst of my sorrows and
tribulations.

Indeed, you are the Mother of mercy, and you give to the sinner
hope of pardon.

Your tenderness, O Mary, and your goodness surpass all that
can be expressed here below.

You are elevated above the glory, above the honors which the
saints possess, higher than the virtues, the benignity, the sweetness and the charm of blessed spirits.

And if it were not thus, O Mary, how could you inundate the
unfortunate with so much sweetness, with so many consolations, with such great hope, and such great contrition.

You will never be impoverished, for in you is conceived the
   Source of all goodness,
You are the ornament of the heavens, and the joy of the Saints,
   and you are the tabernacle of the Holy of Holies.
Our forefathers longed for you for aeons. You, the chosen
   mother and the elected virgin, who were to grant all pardon on
   earth and all fullness in heaven.

(Three Tabernacles, Chap. III)

HOMILY

IMAGES AND RESEMBLANCES BETWEEN THE MOTHER AND THE CHILDREN

I.   The images and the figures of Mary, in history and in life, are given to make us love and admire our Mother, but also to recall to us that we ought to resemble her. The resemblance, even physical, between the mother and the children, is a fact of adaptation as much as of race. We can by contemplation arrive at this resemblance which belongs to the children of the same mother.

II.   If we do not achieve a perfect resemblance, we can at least, achieve a general reproduction of the model which makes an image of it. Scripture gives of Mary the sweetest and the most grandiose images. She is the dwelling of God, the garden of delights, the gate of heaven, the morning star, the health of the sick, the refuge of sinners. She is grace and sweetness; she is the dream and the realization of all tenderness.

III.   This is the canticle of the heart; this is the cantilena of poetry which we repeat to her with the author of the Scripture, in greeting her as an admirable mother.

MEDITATION

THE MODEL AND THE IMITATOR

The model, in painting, is a subject contemplated and loved, which the artist tries to reproduce as exactly as he can, or at least, to imitate in its general outlines.

In like manner we ought to act in contemplating Mary. In order to form ourselves to her image, it is necessary to transform ourselves, for she is beauty and we are ugliness. She is formed from a particle of the divinity whereas we are fashioned from a clod of clay.

But the clay is malleable and the divine imprint puts in it a bit of light and of fire, when it permits itself to be penetrated. Therefore let us open our hearts, let us open our souls to the influence of grace. It is so much the easier to do so since we are in the arms of a mother.

Practice: To meditate each day on a mystery of the Rosary: *Contemplare et mirare.*

Thought: The more we resemble Mary the closer we are to God.

CHAPTER X

THE DIVINE MATERNITY OF MARY

I.

A new marvel appears in creation: by the power of God a woman encompasses the Creator in her flesh.

What is this marvel, O Lord Jesus, but your conception by the Holy Ghost and your nativity of the Virgin Mary?

It is the nativity not yet understood here below, it has not had a parallel, it will never have an equal.

O holy and truly blessed nativity which puts to flight the ancient sin, and which brings to the world a new sanctity.

Rise, new Mother; sing, O Mary, you are the woman spoken of by the prophet, you are she who by her maternity merits this ineffable glory, this indescribable glory, for you have borne within your womb, O Immaculate One, enclosed in your virginal flesh Him whom the whole world knows not how to contain:

You have thus become more than the whole universe.

For this Divine Child who made Himself your Son, directly from your womb already appears to us a man, if not by the grandeur of His created body at least by the virtue of His hidden divinity.

Yea, your Son, Jesus, O Blessed Mother, from the moment of His conception, was already replete with grace and truth.

II.

Speak then, O Lady, speak to your servant, for your servant listens!

You are my sovereign, Mary, and much more, I say it with confidence, you are my mother, and Jesus, your Son, has become my brother.

Truly, you have brought Him forth, not to keep Him for yourself alone, but to give Him to the world.

No longer do I wish to give the name of mother to any other but you, Mary, because you are the Mother of God and my mother.

There is not here below a woman equal to you in power, in grandeur, in beauty, in meekness, in charity, in sweetness, in compassion, in fidelity, nor in love.

III.

I desire, today, to choose you for my mother, and I desire, Mary, to confide myself entirely to you.

I would desire that this choice might be confirmed by you forever; for it suffices for me, Mary, to be able to be united to you for all time.

I shall then greatly rejoice in your name, and I shall magnify your praises for all eternity, O Mary.

(The Valley of Lilies, Chap. VII)

HOMILY

THE FUNCTIONS OF THE MOTHER

I. The role of the mother is not only to give life but to embellish it. A portion of her being is transmitted through the mother to the child. This is the marvel of creation which is renewed.

The spiritual filiation also has something of this creation. That is why the children of Mary bear within themselves a ray of heaven. As Jesus, who was formed from the flesh of Mary, we can be formed from her heart. Mary is truly the Mother of God: *Theotókos*, she who has brought forth God, as the Greek Church says. But she is also the Mother of men, *Mater viventium*, as the Latin Church calls her.

II. After having brought us forth to the life of grace, Mary helps us to perfect in ourselves this supernatural life. Perfection is composed of a harmonious whole; the smallest defect detracts from the model. Therefore it is necessary to resolve to make all imperfections disappear. Do we always think of that?

III. The author asks Mary to help him to attain this end and to realize this wish: to resemble his Mother.

MEDITATION

MATERNAL AND FILIAL TENDERNESS

The love of a father is an act of force, stirring and active; the love of a mother is an act of compassion, vibrant and passive which bears a special name, tenderness.

Tenderness is a love composed of inclination and attentions. It is all sweetness and grace, it is feminine.

If the heart of a mother is thus, the heart of a child is the same. Our love for a father differs from our love for a mother. Our love for a father is, most often, an act of reflection; our love for a mother is always an impulse of the heart.

So it is in the spiritual life. It is that which always makes devotion to Mary something gentle and sweet, something which comes from the heart. In other words, we live more by the heart than by the mind.

Practice: To keep and look at images and medals with faith.

Thought: One must think of a mother so as to overcome temptations.

PART TWO

SORROWFUL MYSTERIES

Chapter XI

THE PIOUS PATRONAGE OF MARY

I.

Happy is he who knows how to accept in this life,
both Jesus and Mary, and the angels and the saints,
for guides on the way and counsellors in doubt,
for masters at work and directors in repose,
for companions at home and friends when abroad,
for aids in combat and helpers in dangers,
for patrons at death and judges at judgment,
for intercessors with God and co-heirs to heaven.

You, who wish to leave the world and its attractions,
let Jesus and Mary be your only loves:
let God be your Father and Jesus your brother;
let Mary, henceforth, be your only Mother.

Take the angels for your friends, the unfortunate for your
brothers, the humble and the poor for your companions.

II.

There is the holy family and the fruitful race that God creates
for you, and that He loves.

It has faith for a foundation, hope for its strength, patience and
charity for its ornaments.

Tremble and sing, faithful soul, as Mary once sang before God,
trembling on the day of her great joy when the Saviour, Jesus,
was conceived in her.

Praise the Lord, praise Him lavishly and say to Mary: I find
refuge today near you, my mother, and beg humbly your
support.

III. Prayer:

If you are with us in the struggle, Mary, who then will dare to rise against us?

And if you give us your protection, who then will ever be able to repulse us?

Extend over me, extend your arms, Mary, because I wish to seek my refuge in your shadow.

Say to my soul: I am your advocate, fear nothing. As a mother consoles her son, thus I shall console you, my child.

How sweet are your words, Mary, and how your voice consoles me, Mother!

Allow my heart always to hear it.

(Devout Prayers, Prayer III)

HOMILY

THE INFLUENCE OF A WOMAN AND A MOTHER IN THE WORLD

I. The remembrance, like the presence of a mother, is the most powerful incentive to goodness in the world. The life of civilized peoples is entirely organized to please the woman. Poetry, art, style, all are made for her. One can also say that it is she who brings forth poetry and art, when she knows how to inspire them.

From this point of view the influence of Mary is found manifested in the most beautiful masterpieces of architecture and of painting in the world. Nothing is beautiful in life without the mother.

II. Woman possesses an additional charm when she is a mother. The history of peoples is full of heroic recitals and beautiful actions accomplished through maternal love. Neither the Greeks nor the Romans would have arrived at the degree of civilization and of beauty which we admire, without the cult of maternity.

The Christian religion is greater, more beautiful and more alluring in proportion as the cult of Mary, the mother and the ideal woman, is developed and inscribed in practice and in art.

MEDITATION

THE POWER OF A WOMAN

Instinctively, from her very nature itself, woman loves to protect and to embrace in order to defend and attract others to herself. The power of a woman is in her attraction and in her function; whereas the power of a man is in his strength only. The ancients had symbolized these functions by giving to kings a scepter of iron and to queens a scepter of flowers. The one dominates by his force, the other by her graciousness.

Nothing resists the power of graciousness; a smile can break or transform a life. Let the Christian woman use this power for good. Piety, says St. Francis de Sales, ought to make a woman more gracious, for she ought to possess both supernatural grace and natural graciousness.

Practice: Try to reproduce, even exteriorly, the royal grace of Mary.

Thought: Mary is beauty and grace: *Speciosa et formosa.*

CHAPTER XII

THE DELIGHTS OF MARY

I.

No language on this earth will be able to express the delights and joys of the Virgin Mary.

No mind will ever be able to comprehend the abundance of her joys as virgin, the greatness of her consolations as mother:

For, the more abundant is the infusion of grace, the more numerous also are the gifts of happiness. In like manner, the more frequent are the visits of God, the more ardent, too, are desire and love.

Imitate, therefore, the Mother of the Saviour, so as to be numbered among her children.

Try attentively to walk in the steps of Mary on the road of virtue, in order to attain to glory with her.

II.

Have intense grief for your past lukewarmness, for your faults, alas! not yet overcome.

Pray that all creatures may glorify God and observe His laws.

Give thanks for the divine benefits granted through the Mother of God.

Render to her all honor and all reverence; for, if the natural law obliges children to love their mother according to the flesh, how much more ought we to testify affection and show tenderness to the Mother of grace?

It is a duty to love above all mothers Mary who is, at the same time, Mother of God, Mother of Holy Church, and our own Mother.

III. Prayer:

How shall I ever be sad of heart when you give your consolation, Mary?

How could one fear the enemy, one who can, at each moment, have recourse to you?

Incline, O Mother filled with tenderness, incline your ears to my humble prayers.

Incline, O Mother filled with tenderness, like Rebecca, toward your servant, and give him a few drops to drink.

Pour into me a part, however small it may be, of that grace and of that sweet consolation which is mysteriously hidden in you.

This grace is at all times desirable for all persons, it is always pleasant to receive; it is indispensable for me at this moment.

The smallest drop placed on lips by you, Mary, seems to me so powerful and so great in its excellence, that all other pleasures on earth seem vile, without value, and equal to nothing.

(The Devout Prayers, Prayer III)

HOMILY

Joys and Christian Pleasures

Joy is a sentiment which enlarges the heart and makes it beat more strongly. Joy dilates, exalts and magnifies. Sadness, on the contrary, contracts and diminishes life.

I.   Mary who had in life so many causes of sadness and so many kinds of grief, is nevertheless called by Scripture: the Mother of holy happiness, *Mater pulchrae laetitiae*. Happiness is a virtue which breaks out into joy, to delight others. It is therefore an act of virtue which supposes an effort and a gift of one's self.

II.   Mary, more than any other creature, possessed this gift and practised this virtue. Christian art, like religious history, shows us always the Virgin in the midst of flowers, beaming with light. It is a representation, but a representation full of serene reality.

III.   We are attracted by this serenity and the heart is caught in the divine contemplation. Let us ask, as a grace, the joy and the happiness of the heart, so that we may pour them forth through christian joys which dilate the souls.

MEDITATION

A Good Character

The character is formed as any habit of virtue is formed. To have a good character is to be on the road of perfection.

A good character is first of all, *character*, that is to say, firm and stable and not changeable and variable. It is in the second place, *good*, which means, pleasing to others.

Only the people who breathe joy have a good character. The people who are glum in everything, as is said in current language, are never of an agreeable character. They are a burden to others and to themselves.

Form your character so that it may be stable. Refine it, so that it may be gentle. Conquer it so that it may be usable.

You will then be, like to Mary, exultant with joy and glorifying God in your life every day.

Practice: To form character, it is often necessary to know how to break it, by doing that which pleases the least.

Thought: *Gaude et laetare, Virgo Maria.* Rejoice and be glad, O Mary!

CHAPTER XIII

THE EXULTATIONS OF MARY

I.

My soul has exulted before God, my Saviour. Exult again and again, Mary, because you give to the world the joy of its salvation.

Rejoice, O Immaculate Mother, because you preserve the honor of virginity.

Exult with happiness, virgin made mother, because you preserve the honor of virginity, from the maledictions which weigh upon women.

You can surely rejoice before God. Him whom the earth and heaven united, could not contain, you have within you.

You warm Him in your arms, you place Him joyfully in His crib, you alone, Mother, can adore Jesus, your Son, born of you in time, He who, before you, before all time, possesses God as Father from all eternity.

You alone fulfill the duties of a mother to the God who confers maternity on you.

You alone can truly exult in Him who renders you sublime and heavenly.

II.

Let heaven and earth praise you, Mary, let every creature re-echo your praises!

Let my whole being rejoice in your presence, let my soul exalt you, beloved mother!

The tongue is powerless to speak of your grandeurs, and the spirit to conceive the wonder of you.

Thus, I can only bow before you humbly and say to you prayerfully: receive me in your arms, O my Mother, listen with love to the sighs of my heart, and receive with me all who are mine.

My soul is breathless at the sight of Jesus, since it knows that in Him alone is found its happiness.

Show me this mysterious treasure which you keep hidden within you, Mary!

Yes, I believe that He is the only-begotten Son of the Father, and I also believe that He is your first-born, mysteriously born of your virginity.

I know that He is my God, my Saviour, and my Father, and I know that He chose you for His mother,

Oh! I wish through you to see Him, your Son, and I wish to adore Him in your arms.

O Mother, you have clothed Him in your flesh. Hence He can not be seen without your aid.

And if you do not deign to show Him to us, who will ever merit to look upon Him?

Through you alone we have access to the Son, and through the Son we shall reach the Father.

Therefore, show me Jesus: He satisfies my soul. I do not seek nor desire a Father other than Jesus, your Son, my Saviour and my God.

O Mother, I have longed with such desire to see Jesus whom you love more than all others!

My soul sighs and longs to contemplate Him, my heart rejoices and seeks to possess Him!

If you wish with Mary to see Jesus, you must, first of all, have pure eyes.

If you wish with Mary to see Jesus, you must ,secondly, be holy and pious.

If you wish with Mary to see Jesus, you must, finally, abandon the earth and strive to rise, little by little, to heaven.

III. Prayer:

O Mary, I know my sins and my failings. I know that I am unworthy to see Jesus,

But I am unable to rest until I have contemplated Him.

Neither can I forbear to plead, for I know He wishes to be asked.

My heart urges me to insist, for I know that you, too, wish that we ask.

Thus, O my Mother, I desire to persevere in prayer and contemplation.

(Sermons on the Nativity, Sermon II)

HOMILY

GREAT MANIFESTATIONS OF JOY

Christian virtue not only does not exclude joys, but necessitates great social and familiar manifestations of them, which constitute the charm of life.

I. It is not without effort that one succeeds in accomplishing these acts. A sad saint is a poor saint, says St. Francis of Sales. The source of joy, like the cause of happiness, lies in the similarity of life to action. To do nothing is to be sad. The more one acts, the more the heart dilates. It soars, it is inflamed, it is exalted.

II. The true cause of sincere manifestations of joy, which enrich the life of families and societies, is Jesus Himself. Without Him there is no real joy; outside of Him no serenity. See the people without religion and the people without belief. All is sombre among them and all breathes boredom.

III. Let us not be like this. Let us approach Mary and look upon Jesus. This will in itself be a lesson and an attraction.

MEDITATION

SERENITY AND A SMILE

A calm woman is a queenly woman, says an old proverb. Gentleness and calmness, a smile and graciousness are, truly, the force and strength of a woman. Too often they are represented as faults and perverted attractions. This is an error and a falsehood.

To know how to make use of these attractions and of these graces can also be and ought to be for a woman, a virtue and a practice of Christian life. The man who has once encountered such attractions is captivated forever. The prayer that the Church offers in nuptial Masses asks for the woman these virtues of grace and beauty.

Practice: To smile and to be gracious in all the circumstances of life.

Thought: You are, Mary, the most beautiful of women:
Speciosa et decora inter filias Jerusalem.

CHAPTER XIV

MARY'S LOVE AND SORROW

I.

The Infant Jesus remained at Jerusalem after the Pasch and was lost; and His parents did not at first perceive it on their return.

Oh unexpected change! oh mystery! Would it not have been better to remain at Nazareth and not to lose the Child while traveling?

Truly so, because to lose Jesus is to have lost more than the whole universe and all that it contains.

Alas! how could there be a festival for the parents experiencing so harrowing a trial.

For there is no misfortune more dreadful for the sad and afflicted, than to lose that which may alone serve as a consolation to them.

Only those who know what it is to love are able to comprehend the depth of the Virgin Mary's grief in this trial.

Much more willingly she might have remained in solitude, hidden at Nazareth, rather than present herself in Jerusalem so as to appear in the Temple for the solemnities.

But she, the Mother of the Law, wished to observe fully the customs and the law in order to give us an example of obedience.

Besides, she left her home and her village thus to present herself according to the prescribed custom at Jerusalem with Jesus and Joseph.

II.

Likewise, it was to give us a model of patience in grief that God permitted Mary to lose her Son, that after having lost Him she might seek Him weeping; that she might find Him only after three days, and that after having found Him, she might more joyfully take back with her her Treasure.

Let none dare to rely upon himself as if he possessed Christ alone for himself.

Let no one scorn others, for he knows not if he himself is pleasing to God.

Thus Jesus remains hidden for many and manifests Himself only to a few.

He showed His Divinity when He wished, and when He wished He hid Himself, acting always with a purpose and for a reason.

To lose Jesus is not always astonishing; but I feel that it is a misfortune for me, a misfortune alas, deeply felt in my heart.

I recognize, however, that it is through my fault, and that I often deserve still greater affliction because I have not always known how to watch over my heart.

I have been full of negligence and lukewarmness. Thus have I lost the grace of my God and I do not know who shall ever be able to return it to me.

III. Prayer:

Come then to my aid in this great sorrow, O Mother of God and Mother of Mercy.

Help me, divine Mistress Mary, you who give access in heaven to Life. I seek in you peace and happiness.

You know how sorrowful it is to lose Jesus, and also how sweet to find Him again.

If this trial was sent to you, Mary, to you who were sinless, what wonder if it is imposed upon me who so often have offended my God?

What must I do to find Jesus again?

Oh, if there is for me any hope of finding Him once more, it is in your help that I have placed my hope, O Mary.

It is in your aid and in your merits, you who are more cherished and nearer to Him than any one else.

Teach me then to seek my Beloved until I have found Him. O Mary, accompany me yourself.

Then shall I chant joyously with you: "Congratulate me for I have found my Beloved, the Beloved of my heart, He for whom my soul longs."

(Finding of Jesus in the Temple, Sermon II)

HOMILY

Suffering and Love

To love is to suffer, says Ecclesiastes. However the only thing that one seeks in love is to not suffer, or rather, in true love is to not make the beloved to suffer.

I. But in order to love truly it is requisite to know how to suffer royally. Mary can be our model in this delicate art which sculptures the soul, so to speak, like the blows of a hammer fashion a work of art in marble. Who more than she has loved? Who has suffered more?

II. How has she suffered? As queen, as mother, and as woman; with dignity, with patience, with amenity. To know how to understand the griefs of Mary is to know how to imitate them. One word translates well this state, it is the word, compassion. If Jesus has suffered and undergone His Passion, Mary has known, near to Him, the union in His sufferings and His Passion; this is compassion.

III. Let us retain this word in our life. Let us keep this example before our eyes. Let us know how to suffer and to love like Mary and with Mary.

MEDITATION

Maternal Love

There is no gentler love; there is no stronger love. But is this indeed love? This is more than love, in the common meaning of this word; but it is also less than love.

Maternal love is born of love itself; it is as the flower and the fruit. But love itself is the root and trunk of this beautiful tree which embellishes the earthly paradise.

Love is, furthermore, very beautiful and very attractive only by the fruits which it brings forth and the flowers which it causes to bloom in the soul of the father and mother.

Paternity and maternity are inherent in all love which is born in the heart of man and woman. It is this which enlarges and elevates this beautiful sentiment and this powerful drive, which nothing on earth resists. Mary knew more than any other mother, the force and tenderness of this love. Joseph knew all its delicacies and felt all its charms.

Practice: To love Mary as one loves one's mother.

Thought: Immaculate Heart of Mary, I love you!

CHAPTER XV

SEEKING CHRIST
AFTER THE COUNSELS OF MARY

I.

Listen to my advice, imitate my example, O my son, and you will be consoled.

If it happens sometimes that you lose Christ, do not despair, do not give up, do not cease to give yourself in prayer, do not seek earthly consolation; remain in solitude and weep for yourself; then only will you find Jesus once again, you will find Him in the temple of your heart.

No, it is not at the crossroads of the city, nor in the gatherings of those who amuse themselves, nor among earthly reunions, that Jesus is found; but certainly only in the midst of the just, and in the company of the saints.

II.

It is in tears, O my son, that you must seek Him whom you have lost in pleasures.

It is by faithful service that you must attract Him whom you have deserted by negligence.

It is by humility that you must recall Him whom you have driven afar by pride.

It is by prayer that you must draw Him who does not listen to a heedless heart.

It is with fear and trembling that you should pray to Him who loves not pride and laziness.

It is with gratitude that you should praise Him who is ever ready to give His grace.

It is with an ardent love that you must love Him who loves everyone and pardons everyone, who gives His graces to all without regret, who has never abandoned anyone.

III. Prayer:

O Mary, O Mother, when the gates of heaven are closed because of my sins, when on all sides entrance is forbidden to me, when all strength and all counsel abandon me, when I am unable to aid myself in anything, when the weariness of life and grief of heart overwhelm me to the point of no longer loving anything, when the sun of joy is changed into a night of mourning, when consolations from on high vanish, and when despair presses in upon me from every part, when the wind of temptations arises, and the waves of passion grow stronger, when illness itself overpowers me, when all adversities gather and fight against me, where shall I flee and to whom shall I turn, if it is not to you, Mary, who alone knows how to console the unfortunate and to succour the wretched? Toward whom then shall I turn to attain unhindered, the haven of salvation, to whom if not to you, Mary, Star of the Sea, who shines always in the firmament, who always offers the flaming torch of grace.

(Soliloquy of the Soul, Chap. VI)

HOMILY

Boredom and Sorrow in the Christian Life

I. Life is a strange mixture of joys and sadnesses. To him who knows how to weigh everything well, it seems that joy is superior to sadness. But boredom and sorrows leave in the human heart a sharper imprint than does joy, besides we feel them with greater keenness. The more tender and delicate the heart is, the more keen are its sufferings. Mary, who possessed a nature more refined than any other creature, must have felt physical griefs and moral sufferings with greater sharpness.

II. Anguish, terror, fright, fear, disquietude, boredom, all the griefs of the heart met in her from Bethlehem to Calvary. All the sufferings, poverty, worries, abandonment, long waits, disturbing vigils, all the sorrows of a mother's heart came to assail her. She bore them all with firmness, calmness, and serenity.

III. There is no lesson more engaging for us, there is no model more consoling. Let us look at Mary. Let us listen to Mary, our Mother and exemplar.

MEDITATION

Disquietude and Worry

Among the sorrows of the heart, disquietude and worry are the two most frequent and the two most painful for us and also for those who surround us.

The disturbed person is capable of nothing: *irrequietus*, said the Latins, that is to say, without basis and without support. The worrier is absorbed by his worry and sees nothing else.

To cure one's self of the malady, it is first of all necessary to know how to reflect and to think, and secondly to will and to act. Work, better than anything else, dissipates worries. Besides, it procures a recovery through the result obtained by effort.

Effort: everything depends on it in the life of the soul as in the life of the body; *age quod agis,* do well what you do, said the Proverb from experience, and you will succeed.

Who better than Mary could give us a model and a lesson? Study her; imitate her.

Practice: Never to allow our cares or worries to appear, but to show ourselves ever serene before the world.

Thought: Let us be to others as we would wish to see them be to us.

CHAPTER XVI

THE GRIEFS AND SUFFERINGS OF MARY

I.

Mary did not live a single day without suffering; nevertheless in the midst of her greatest sufferings she was never without consolation.

Every grief borne for Jesus brings to the soul sweetness and joy.

The more we suffer under the weight of the blows, the more we merit the favors of grace.

Yes, Mary suffered, and suffered sorrowfully, because of the sins of the great mass of men.

She suffered in like measure with the just, with those tried by temptations and troubles.

She suffered for the ingratitude of men to whom God sent His Son in order to reopen the lost Paradise; and for the obstinate loss of the wicked who prefer to heaven things of this earth, and who refuse to listen to the Word of God.

She suffered to see the just oppressed; the impious, far from God, everywhere victorious; the poor scorned and the rich exalted.

She suffered to see in all places lukewarmness brought to the service of God, and the haste which offended Him.

She suffered to see the world given over to evil, refusing to turn its eyes toward the light that God Himself came to bring into the world.

These sorrows were like piercing blades sheathed in this Mother's compassionate heart.

Yet, she was patient - always, suffering in silence a life of martyrdom, weeping for the salvation of men.

II.

If you wish to look deeper into her life, you will see what she suffered at the Passion. Meditating on her life you will find that she tasted as many draughts of bitterness as moments lived by Jesus upon this earth, and as many as He had members transpierced on the Cross. When had Jesus suffered an injury without Mary having felt its fulfillment? If she suffered severely when she lost Him for a few days in the Temple, how much more keenly must she have agonized when she saw Him dying, nailed to the Cross?

It is a fact known by all hearts which live, that a mother's love surpasses in compassion all known loves and affections. If, therefore, you wish to penetrate deeply the sorrow of the mother in Mary, think of the excellence and the depth of her virginal love.

III. Prayer:

Come, O Mary, tender and gentle Mother, to pay a visit to my soul in its tribulation.

You alone can give peace, for you alone know how to bring sweetness to the sufferings of the heart. Come, extend your hand to the fallen servant, come, lift him up again by grace. Hasten, O Mary, chosen Mother of God, to show to us all once more the abundance of your piety.

You see me, fallen so low, yet I have not forgotten you, nor shall I ever forget you, O my Mother.

(Sermon to the Novices, Sermon XXV)

HOMILY

SICKNESS AND SUFFERING

I. Among human sorrows, illness has sufferings and sadnesses like to no others. It destroys the body at the same time that it gnaws at the soul. Mary knew, at the foot of the Cross, the most agonizing suffering and the most violent torment. We do not read that she suffered illness properly so-called. Her immaculate body should not have experienced our infirmities. Death itself was for Mary a dormition rather than a consumption.

II. But if Mary did not suffer illness, she had to endure all other sufferings: rendings of the heart, the bitterness of separation, the anguish of uncertitude. Let us learn from her to bear them courageously, if not lovingly. It is necessary to possess the soul of Mary and the heart of St. Therese in order to say with faith: "Either to suffer or to die." More willingly we say: "To live and to rejoice."

III. Let us ask Mary, Queen, Virgin and Martyr, as the Church calls her, to tell us to bear the sorrows of illness with the calmness of a queen, with the gentleness of a virgin, with the strength of a martyr.

MEDITATION

GRIEFS OF THE HEART

The griefs of the heart are sometimes those which are self-created. They are, at other times, imposed upon us. They always rend and harm both body and soul.

It is in these circumstances that it is necessary to know how to look on high, to look to the cross and to look to Mary at the foot of the Cross.

Stabat: Mary stood and did not succumb, St. John tells us. This is a model and a support. Mary is a mother who gives both example and strength to him who knows how to contemplate her.

Practice: To offer to Mary the sufferings and agonies of the heart.

Thought: Immaculate Heart of Mary, make my heart like yours.

Chapter XVII

THE BITTERNESS OF MARY

I.

She remained alone at the foot of the Cross, she stood alone, Mary, the Mother of Jesus, as the Apostle tells us in his divine account.

After the memory of the Cross of Jesus, the most beautiful memory is that of Mary, His Mother, who alone had the courage to remain standing near her Son dying on the Cross, dying to save the world from death.

O moving spectacle of Mother and Son:
>   of the Mother who suffers, and the Son who consoles;
>   of the Mother who weeps and the Son who smiles;
>   of the Mother who remains standing near the Cross, and
>   of the Son attached to that same Cross;
>   of the Mother who sighs and the Son who dies.

O immensity of grief, worthy to remain ever imprinted in the heart of Christians.

II.

Pilate wrote on wood for the Cross, this title: Jesus of Nazareth, King of the Jews.

You also write, but write on your heart this title, against the derisions of men and against the subtle assaults of the devil.

By the sheer force of this Name you will be delivered from all the attacks of the wicked.

Act thus and engrave in your heart this title of Jesus, suspended on the Cross. You will then find near you Mary, standing as at the Cross, interceding for you in time of temptation and at the hour of death.

III.

No mother in this world in giving birth to a beloved child felt a happiness equal to that of Mary, who alone had for a Son the same Son as God.

No mother experienced a sorrow equal to that of Mary, at the death of her Son.

Mary had to suffer in her compassion all the sorrows of her Son in the Passion.

Indeed she stood near the Cross in tears, her heart feeling at every grief the pain of a sword which transpierced it with bitterness.

It was truly a marvel that she was able to support in her virginal body a like suffering; for her soul experienced at each torture, a torture equal to that of her Son.

O ineffable martyrdom, ineffable grief of a mother, more cruelly agonized in her heart at the sight of her dying Son, than a martyr in his body overwhelmed by torment.

IV. Prayer:

O Mother, I know that I am not worthy to lift my eyes to your admirable face, to this holy face haloed by glory, which the angels of heaven wonder at on their knees. You appear to me, O Mother, as adorned with deep-hued roses and foliage of gold, and I remain frightened by my impurity.

However, O Mary, because of your goodness I retain in spite of everything, the assured hope of obtaining once more the grace of pardon if you deign to intercede again for me.

What may I wish, expect, or desire to obtain from the most indulgent of mothers, as from the most compassionate of virgins, if it is not pardon and consolation in the calmness and joy of a sincere repentance?

(Monastic Enchiridion, Chap. V)

HOMILY

Sufferings and Tears

I. The Gospel which speaks to us often of Mary's sufferings, never says that she wept; it does say it however of Jesus, *lacrymatus est*. Mary, too, must have wept. Tears are an alleviation of the heart. But tears ought not to cast one down.

II. To suffer is a science. It requires a heart which feels grief very strongly, which bleeds and which exalts, but which knows how to conquer itself and to submit itself to reason and to faith.

III. O Mary, be our model in sufferings and in tears! Be also our support and our consolation.

MEDITATION

Ennui and Lassitude

Nothing is more deplorable in the spiritual life as in natural life, than ennui. Nothing is more weakening and nothing is more discouraging than this feeling. It is necessary, at any price, to struggle against this encroachment which little by little destroys life itself and which renders it painful to itself and to others. Ennui engenders lassitude and lassitude produces inertia and death.

A soul which is weary is a soul which does not act. To fight ennui, first of all it is requisite to work. The Latins call ennui by a name which recalls death: *taedium*.

Let us flee this as one flees a plague which threatens to communicate itself. Thus is Mary called in Scripture, the Mother of holy joy: *Mater sanctae laetitiae*.

Practice: Never to make others feel the difficulties we may have.

Thought: O Mary, be our happiness and our joy: *causa nostrae laetitiae*.

CHAPTER XVIII

HOW TO SUFFER
AFTER THE EXAMPLE OF MARY

I.

If you truly love your mother Mary, and if you truly desire her patronage in the midst of your own tribulations, remain with her standing near the Cross.

Share with a full heart in her mother's sorrows and in the sorrows of Christ, her beloved Son: she will then be near you at the hour of death.

He who often and lovingly meditates on the sorrows borne by Jesus, and on the tears shed by His mother, can have full confidence in the mercy and pity of God, and likewise in His affection and in that of His divine Mother!

Oh! how happy at the hour of death will be that soul which on every day of its life loved deeply both Jesus and Mary, and each day found its place near the Cross, in union with Jesus and Mary!

II.

Happy the one who, scorning all earthly consolation, chose in this life Mary for his consolation and his mother.

There is no doubt that at the hour of his death, this mother will say to her Son the blessed and gentle word that consoles the poor and helps the orphan.

III.

If you love Jesus, come, take up His cross; walk with the cross; remain near the cross; embrace this cross and do not forsake it until you have arrived near the One who gives the glory to the cross.

If you wish in your trials, in spite of the sorrow, to find some consolation, go to Mary at once both virgin and mother, to the mother who watches near the cross; to the virgin who weeps at the foot of the cross.

All suffering will then disappear for you, or at least, will seem lighter and more bearable compared to the griefs of the Virgin Mary.

IV. Prayer:

I come again to ask you Mary, Mother of God and my mother, to be willing to look upon me favorably, and to consider me with a compassionate heart, now, in the future, and at the hour of death.

Receive me as a son under your protection; enfold me maternally in your arms at all times, but especially at my last hour.

Remember me, and come to my aid, you who are my sovereign and my mother.

Console my soul affrighted at itself, O you, my sole hope in my tribulations.

Defend it against the assaults of the demon, so that he will never dare to approach it, in the presence of you who deign to visit it.

Obtain for me, Mary, I plead with you, through your pious intercession pardon and indulgence from your Son, whom I have so often and so greatly, alas! offended by my faults and my sins.

(Garden of Roses, Chap. IV)

HOMILY

Endurance and Resignation

I. There are in man two forces, a positive which is action, and a negative which is resignation. To endure without weakening necessitates resignation. But the resignation ought not to be an oppression; resignation is a virtue, and weakness is a defect.

II. You must know how to suffer and be resigned, but like Mary, with strength and magnanimity, that is to say, with a great soul and a great will. Suffering thus borne purifies and does not weaken one. Do we know how to suffer thus?

III. Let us ask Mary to teach it to us, to support us in the apprenticeship of life. Patience, in the original sense of the word, means the science of suffering. Let us ask for this science through the intercession of our Mother.

MEDITATION

An undesirable character is an illness; the spirit which is subject to bad humor is ill and communicates to the body its illness.

An undesirable character is variable, cross-grained, changeable, capricious, and brutal. It lacks poise and circumspection.

A character, on the contrary, becomes good when it is strong, well-balanced, constant, unvariable. Not to change with every wind is to possess strength of character, it is to approach God who is immutable in goodness.

To make firm your character, it is necessary to refine your spirit and to harden your body to suffering. *Fortiter agi et pati*, said the Stoics. The Christian, marked by the cross, should know better how to say this, and still better how to practice it.

Practice: Render your character tractable by accustoming yourself to prompt obedience.

Thought: To act always forcefully and energetically: *Fortiter age.*

Chapter XIX

HOW ONE MUST SERVE JESUS AFTER MARY'S EXAMPLE

I.

Who are the highest in heaven, and who were the most humble on this earth among the creatures endowed with life?

Is it not Jesus? Is it not Mary?

Jesus made Himself for us the servant of all, and Mary calls herself a servant.

The earth proclaims the grandeur and the heavens in chorus sing the sublime dignity of Jesus and Mary, here below and on high.

Oh, you may unite your voice to these voices, to sing the sweet names of Jesus and Mary!

It is also good to put yourself in the service of those who have made themselves our servants.

Indeed, serve the Lord, you sons of men, serve Him who first deigned to serve you.

Serve Mary too: she gave you the example of being humble and of giving service.

It is a duty for you and it is to your advantage to honor before all, these two powerful models.

You must pray to them daily, even hourly, because they have the power to conquer the enemy and to procure the joys of victory.

II.

Thus, in every condition hurry to Jesus and, at the same time, hurry to Mary.

Expose to them always your needs and your troubles.

Confess your sins and weep for your forgetfulness: arouse your hope and wait for grace.

If you fall, alas! with facility, hasten to rise all the more quickly. Sincere prayers are always listened to and true pleadings are always heard.

The angels in their turn will rejoice for you on seeing you cleansed from the ugliness of sin.

For your part, avoid sin henceforth. Mary will obtain for you the pardon of Jesus.

Pray to Jesus and Mary for the honor that is due to them: Jesus and Mary will then give you assistance and courage.

III. Prayer:

It is to you, O Jesus, my Lord and my God, to you, O Mary, Mother of God and my mother, that I wish to confide my body and soul.

You alone are my hope and my help in my troubles and in my tribulations.

Let your tenderness and your affection sustain me everywhere! This is my only prayer.

(Monastic Enchiridion, Chap. IV)

HOMILY

LATENT FORCES IN LIFE

I. There is in each one of us a hidden power, a latent force which is personal, that no other possesses. There are no two souls exactly alike. It is these hidden forces which we must cultivate and exercise in order to arrive at perfection.

II. That is true in the spiritual domain as in the world of matter. Men of genius, the saints, attained this superior state which constitutes heroism, only by putting to work the special forces of their soul, as well as the material dispositions of their body.

III. *Nosce teipsum.* One must know himself to perfect himself each day. Perfection is not the work of a day, but the crowning of a life. Above all, we must ask for perseverance.

MEDITATION

CONTENTMENT WITH ONESELF

There are people who are always discontented with everything and with themselves. Discontent with the happiness of others, discontent with their life and their lot. This is a whim and a defect.

He who, like the Christian philosopher, would care to look well around him, not only above but below, would easily see that he is not just to think thus.

Without reaching the pessimism which says that we must be content with little, it is important to correct ourselves and to judge ourselves better. To underestimate ourselves is not a virtue; humility thus understood would be a defect.

Let us have great confidence in ourselves! Let us enlarge our thought and our affection! He who knows himself well, loves himself; he who loves himself, encourages himself. Let us have confidence in ourselves!

Practice: Never allow yourself to be disheartened by a defeat or a trial.

Thought: If I consider myself, I find myself happy.
Contentus sua sorte, said Socrates.

CHAPTER XX

HOW TO ACT
AFTER THE EXAMPLE OF MARY

I.

My memory will live in the succession of centuries, is said in Ecclesiastes in reference to Mary.

Mary, humble and poor in everything, a model of patience and perfection, from the day of her birth until the hour of her death lived poor and hidden, a life of suffering.

You who suffer, come to her always, and each day search for what you can put at her feet, as at the feet of a mother, in eager token of respect and love.

If you wish to rejoice in heaven with Mary, suffer poverty on earth with Mary.

Take for a model her examples both of poverty and humility.

Flee the vain amusements of men: watch lest you offend by useless words or unworthy acts, either Jesus your God, or Mary your mother.

II.

It is certainly not a simple and slight fault to offend such loving protectors.

They see at all times how you work and how you try to reform yourself; and, depending on your efforts, they regulate their help.

However, their love surpasses your wickedness, and their goodness always incites repentance.

If you realize that you have erred, change your resolution for the better.

Persevere in the good and know how to give thanks for all the gifts received. It is thus that Mary acted in her life of union with Jesus here on earth.

Learn from the example of this goodness to accept the annoyances of life, to submit yourself in everything to the unknown designs chosen for you by God from all eternity.

Jesus will then be for you a protector, and Mary a loving and faithful mother.

Be on your part a devoted child, a faithful servant, always eager for that which is good.

III. Prayer:

I greet you with composure, Virgin full of grace, the Lord is with you!

I greet you, sole hope of the poor!

I greet you, gentle mother of orphans!

I have revealed to you, up until now to you alone, my failings: henceforth I shall reveal them with still more assurance, because I feel that a great virtue flows from you, and that your name exhales a perfume that embalms the heart and comforts the soul.

O sweet name of Mary, name of grace and charm,
name always sweet to say, and sweet to think upon,
name fashioned in heaven,
name carried by the angels,
name recommended by the Gospel to men,
when as if by making of it a eulogy:
the name of the chosen virgin was: Mary!

(Mystical Prayers, Chap. VI)

HOMILY

ACTION AND EFFORT

I. Action is the sign of life; to live is to act, in the domain of the spiritual life, as in the domain of the natural life. But action is not without effort and effort supposes work. Is there a more beautiful example of work than that of Mary? See her in the Temple, at Nazareth, at Jerusalem. See her weaving the seamless robe of the Infant Jesus, in the splendid picture of *Mater admirabilis.*

II. Mary works in prayer and in contemplation. More than that, her work is a prayer. To pray is to lift our soul to God. Work ought not bind us to the earth, but to aid us to rise to heaven, through effort and through the soaring of the heart.

III. But work is hard; labor is harsh. Thus we must join to work, prayer, which itself carries us on the wings of love to the sky, with Mary.

MEDITATION

CHARACTER

Character is that which leaves an indelible imprint on each soul and each individual. In the original sense of the word, character was an impression with a heated iron, on a stipe of wood. The imprint thus marked grows with the tree and remains visible.

It ought to be likewise for the soul. To have character is praiseworthy for any man; to possess character is admirable for a woman. Virtue is nothing more, because virtue is a lasting imprint.

To have character, we must know how to suffer. Let us see in Mary our model and our examplar. What a beautiful type and what a beautiful character, forged of strength and sweetness. From the Crib to Calvary, she appears always beautiful, always good, always strong. Can we imagine a more appealing model? Let us imitate her always.

Practice: Accustom yourself to keep even-tempered in all cir-
            cumstances.

Thought: Often say with Mary: Lord, let it be done to me
           according to Your will.
           Fiat mihi secundum verbum tuum.

PART THREE

GLORIOUS MYSTERIES

CHAPTER XXI

THE INTERIOR LIFE OF MARY

I.

Willingly remain in solitude and silence in order to pray better:

It is thus that Mary dwelt with the angel, alone in her retreat and speaking only with him.

An angel will come likewise to you and will announce to you the marvels of heaven.

He will come likewise as a helper and a guardian, and before him the spirit of evil will flee.

To retire and to be silent after the example of Mary is the only means of having peace of heart, of obtaining from God the gift of prayer.

Watch the bee eager to gather its honey; it passes through the flowers but without attaching itself; scarcely laden with its sugar, it flees hastily toward the hive and hides the honey, so as to be able to enjoy it during the winter in solitude and tranquility.

It thus encloses the fragrance of the perfume for fear that by going forth, flying hither and yonder, it may thus lose the fruit of its work.

II.

Besides, perfumes carefully enclosed in their containers are better preserved.

On the contrary, those which are left open, are not slow to lose their fragrance.

Nor do flowers too often handled delay in losing their freshness.

A flower blooms well only in gardens: it is sheltered behind walls.

Roses born in the shade of the enclosure open quickly and are long fragrant; while those which are sown along the highways lose their odor, wither, and die.

In like manner, a torch lit in high wind is likely to be extinguished; while the light protected by a shade remains burning.

So it is with our devotion; it is conserved and grows in retirement, whereas it evaporates and is lost in noise.

Three things are especially necessary for man; three things are pleasing to God, to Mary and to the angels;
    manual labor to counteract physical desire,
    love of study to counteract heaviness of heart,
    attention in prayer to counteract the art of the demon.

Therefore, love retirement and work often if you wish to have peace of heart.

III. Prayer:

You are sweet and beautiful, O Mary, my mother, holy Mother of God full of grace.

He alone could enumerate your virtues who could enumerate the stars in the heavens.

Just as the visible sky appears above the earth, lofty and sublime, so does your life appear exalted above our lives.

You alone merit to have been chosen from all eternity for the Mother of God.

And of being, in time, consecrated by the Holy Spirit; greeted by angels; instructed by the archangel and overshadowed by the spirit of the Lord.

(The Valley of Lilies, Chap. IV)

HOMILY

THE LIFE OF CONSCIENCE

I. Lacordaire said that in the solitude of the conscience the most beautiful mysteries of life unfold. He who could penetrate the interior of Mary would there contemplate with delight splendor worthy of heaven. It is in solitude and silence that is wrought this intimate life which the mystic calls the interior life. Mary lived it in company with the angels, in the intimacy of Jesus. What models for us! But also what effort!

II. It is by work and concentration that the sap of the corporal life is formed; it is through work and meditation that the food of the spiritual life is produced. Mary gives us a sublime example of it, a notable model which we ought to try to reproduce.

III. This is the grace we ask for in the exultant prayer which recalls the gifts and the interior privileges of the Mother of God, who is also our own mother and model.

MEDITATION

THE LIFE OF THE HEART

To live by the heart is to live doubly. Assuredly, all life flows from the heart, but just as the heart beats more quickly and strongly in the hours of anguish and of love, thus it is the life of the soul.

What we call the life of the heart is the affective life, the ascent of Calvary, the search for perfection. Love and do as you wish, said St. Augustine. This is the philosophy of love and of the interior life.

The heart of Mary, more than any other human heart, knew the tenderness of love and the anguish of grief. Heart of a mother and heart of a woman, heart of a virgin and heart of a martyr, formed in an immaculate flesh and transformed by contact with the Heart of God Himself, since the Heart of Jesus and the heart of Mary exchanged the same blood and lived the same life. Let us place our heart near to hers.

Practice: To search constantly for something to do for the love of your neighbor.

Thought: Heart of Mary, sanctuary of sorrow and of love: *Amori et dolori sacrum.*

Chapter XXII

THE WORKS AND EXAMPLE OF MARY

I.

For my spirit is sweet above honey, and my inheritance above honey and the honeycomb.

It is in all truth that these lovely words, words of eternal wisdom, are said about Mary, the mother of Jesus our Savior.

Jesus is gentle to us; Mary is all sweetness. There is in them neither bitterness nor sadness, but compassion, sweetness, love, and an untiring eternal mercy.

Happy is he who follows the example of Jesus! Happy is he who confides himself to the love of Mary!

He will unfailingly secure help and support from them.

Gather together as souvenirs the actions and words of Jesus while on earth.

What He did, what He said: you will find in these more than all the treasures of the world.

Meditate with equal attention on the words and actions of Mary:

They will be for you a help and a support more pleasing to the heart than balm and perfumes.

II.

Just as the body has need of food in order to live; and perfume in order to be sweet-smelling, so too the soul has need of virtues to keep alive, and of meditations to remain strong.

The more the soul gives itself to elevated matters, the more it confides itself to wise directors, the better it acquires the glorious science of the saints, and the more quickly it attains the joys of the blessed.

Jesus and Mary are for us in every way sublime masters and models of sanctity; keep them constantly before your eyes and be attentive to them.

Unite yourself to them; enter into intimacy with them.

Everywhere that anyone speaks on the mysteries of Jesus our Saviour and of Mary His mother, listen carefully, and think often of what the names of Jesus and Mary hold for you of strength and sweetness.

III. Prayer:

Holy Mary, Mother of God, ever virgin, mother enriched while on earth with so many favors that the mind of man can neither comprehend them nor speak of them in their greatness, behold me before you, I am your servant, humbly prostrate at the foot of your throne, with all the ardor of a heart which knows how to love.

You are elevated above the archangels, holy Mother of God; you deserve to be, because you have been the most humble of women.

You have found grace even in the eyes of God, O Virgin all beautiful and Mother incomparable.

There is not in heaven nor on earth a creature worthy to be compared to you.

Again I kneel humbly at your feet, O Mary, in order to be better able to offer you praises from reverent lips and a sinless heart.

(The Valley of Lilies, Chap. X)

HOMILY

ACTION AND DEVOTION

I. To act, in Latin, is the opposite of to suffer. Action supposes the exercise of the will; inaction, on the contrary, is always a passion or an effacement. As action supposes energy, inaction recalls decay. Admirable actions make beautiful lives. Thus Mary rises above other women through the spirit of her works and the force of her action. Here is a model to reproduce.

II. An effort attempted in order to imitate this model even from afar, is already a meritorious action. The accomplished effort constitutes a virtue and virtue raises, beautifies and transforms. The fruit of this practice is called devotion. True devotion is active, not passive. To devote oneself is to give oneself.

III. In a prayer inflamed with lyricism, the author asks Mary to teach him to act and to devote himself as she acted and devoted herself.

MEDITATION

PERSONAL EFFORT

Effort is an act which costs and which supposes courage and energy: moral courage, civil courage, military courage, all are contained. Effort requires the mastery of oneself, an assured character, and a firm will. Discouragement is the opposite of personal effort. According to Mary's example we must know how to stand firm against difficulties and remain standing in spite of trials. *Stabat:* the Virgin Mary stood at the foot of the Cross, said the Evangelist St. John, who accompanied her there.

This is the attitude which is suitable for an imitator of Mary, who wishes to follow Jesus as far as Calvary, and not only to the breaking of bread.

Practice: Never to change a decision once it has been made.

Thought: To you, O Mother, we offer both our strength and our weaknesses.

CHAPTER XXIII

HOW TO PRAY AND MEDITATE ACCORDING TO MARY'S EXAMPLE

I.

Before undertaking a work of piety, before beginning an ordinary task, lift your heart to heaven; invoke Jesus and Mary and confide yourself to their protection.

Offer to God both yourself and your actions: your works will then become meritorious; they will be, at the same time, pleasing to God, useful to your neighbor, and profitable to yourself.

Let your intention be always pure, and let your will be directed toward the good.

Work in silence and speak rarely, but let your prayer unceasingly rise to God daily through the thrice holy name of Jesus.

Begin here below to chant, to love, to praise Jesus through the intercession of His Mother Mary. Praise often their glory and their name so as to merit to reign with them in heaven.

II.

To praise Jesus is to possess sweetness and charm in your soul: to praise Mary is to possess beauty.

When your soul is happy, sing: when it is sad, pray.

The more often you exercise yourself in praise the more you will feel love deepen within you, and the more you will see devotion grow.

Do not forget: you will not be forgotten. Be attentive, vigilant over yourself, and you will find in this way zeal and attention.

You must bleed from the blows of a trial, you must be weighed down by adversity, in order to experience the joy of union with God and better to appreciate His grace.

Happy is he who knows how to listen to the counsel of Jesus and Mary for his own amendment!

He will find joy if he has known tears, because pity in the divine Heart of Jesus surpasses the horror of our sins, and the heart of Mary is a limitless treasure of mercy and compassion for us.

III. Prayer:

O Mary, receive, at the return of its exile, my poor soul distraught among the perils of this world; lead it yourself to the gate of heaven in order to introduce it to the joys of paradise.

Place me near you and say to Jesus the sweet and consoling word, the word of pardon.

You who have received from the mouth of an angel the gratifying Ave of the salutation, grant me the power often to repeat reverently your name so full of sweetness.

Receive, O Mary, my Queen and Mother, the fervent prayer of your servant and shed upon him from your throne on high, looks of tenderness and mercy.

(The Garden of Roses, Chap. VII)

HOMILY

The Prayer of the Heart

I.   Prayer is a science, but also a virtue. The spirit acts in prayer, just as the heart beats. Without these two elements prayer is an empty formula, whereas it ought to constitute a human act. Nothing is more beautiful than the attitude of the man who prays; nothing is more touching than the sight of a woman at prayer. Look upon the Orantes of the Catacombs.

II.   The model, here below, in prayer, as the exemplar for us of all Christian life, is Mary. The very image of the Orant recalls now and then the portrait of the Mother of God. She prays, arms outstretched, as if to rise on outspread wings.

III.   Is our prayer like this? Is it not too often with us the body alone which prays? Let us ask Mary for the science of prayer and the grace of her protection.

MEDITATION

Meditation

To meditate is a mysterious word which, in the language of the Church, means to reflect and to examine with an aspiration of love. To meditate is not only to think, but also to rise to God. Mary, the Gospel tells us, kept the words of Scripture in her heart. There is the true model of meditation: it is with the heart as much as with the intelligence that we meditate in the mystic life.

Meditation can be brief, provided that it be effective. It ought to be effective in the resolution which it inspires. That is to say that it is destined to prepare action and effort.

Practice: Do not allow a single day to pass without making a meditation.

Thought: O Mary, teach me to meditate as you did!

CHAPTER XXIV

HOW TO HONOR AND GLORIFY MARY

I.

Oh, if you would only progress in the praise and in the love of Jesus!

If you would from day to day serve better His divine Mother and honor her better!

But alas, you are weak, lukewarm, and negligent, often blamable and burdened with numerous sins, unworthy even to name Jesus and Mary. How then can you praise them worthily?

Praise is questionable when seen on the lips of a sinner. Holiness can only be worthily praised by those who are themselves holy, and not by sinners.

What then must you do? Be silent or speak? Wretched are you if you keep silent; wretched if you speak unworthily.

How then should one act in order to find mercy with God and not to merit reproach?

Nothing is better to attract the love of Jesus and the compassion of His divine Mother than to humiliate yourself in all things, and at all times, and to put yourself always in the last place.

Have a lowly opinion of yourself; consider yourself as worth nothing; God will be lenient with you and will pardon you: Mary will pray for you and will console you.

Far from being confounded in their presence, you will, on the contrary, receive, for your praises an abundant and unending reward.

II.

If you can do no better in your life, at least in everything that depends on you let your intention replace the action until you are able to improve.

Let those who are fervent and full of devotion pray fervently and devoutly;

Let those who have little love or ardor offer to Jesus at least the little they have through the hands of Mary, the Mother of the living flame.

Alas! We would be unworthy by ourselves to appear in the
presence of the Mother of God, and to speak in order to pray
worthily before her, if Mary herself did not call sinners to the
consoling assembly of the saints, according to the beloved
word of the royal prophet:
"The poor and needy shall come to praise thy name."

III. Prayer:

Comfort with your holy words, O Mary, my sorrowful soul and
my dejected heart.

Say only one word and once again I shall regain courage from
your consolation.

I do not ask for a difficult or an impossible work, but only that
you might say to my heart and to my soul that intimate word
of encouragement which alone can give back to me joy and
happiness.

I come to you as an abandoned son: receive me with a mother's
smile, O Mary, so that your repentant servant may know that
he has found grace and pardon.

Give me the help that my heart solicits and the consolation that
my soul desires: give them to me without delay, O my mother!

(Sermons to the Novices, Sermon XXV)

HOMILY

HONOR AND HONORS

I. Honor is the sentiment of our own grandeur and the high consideration of our dignity. Honors are only exterior signs of interior value.

After Jesus, no one is greater than Mary. To her alone is offered a cult of hyperdulia, above the cult given to the saints.

II. How can we manifest to her this cult and this devotion? The author tells us how: by enlarging our heart. What does it mean—to enlarge our heart? It means to fill it with sublime sentiments and heroic resolutions.

III. Sanctity is only sustained heroism. Through our own effort we can arrive at this sublime state. Also, let us ask Mary to help us in it with her protection.

MEDITATION

HUMILITY AND HUMILIATION

Humility is sometimes considered as a lowering of oneself by oneself. It is not thus that it should be considered in the spiritual life. Humility would then be humiliation, which is not a virtue.

We can be humiliated by someone; we could practice humility only by ourselves. Therefore humility is the feeling of our own inferiority in relation to God. Mary is proclaimed a humble servant of the Lord, while yet being the Mother of the Savior, the Queen of heaven and earth.

Let us be humble like her, while recognizing our dignity as Christians.

Practice: To habituate yourself never to take offense from the lack of consideration of others for you.

Thought. The Lord exalts the humble, said Mary in her canticle of the *Magnificat*.

CHAPTER XXV

HOW ONE MUST GO TO JESUS
THROUGH MARY

I.

Happy is he who daily comes to offer his homage, his praise, his heart, and his love to Jesus and Mary.

Happy is he who invokes them and seeks them! Oh! what sweetness is there in the name of Jesus! What sweetness also in the name of Mary.

Happy is the pilgrim who in time of exile remembers constantly his fatherland on high, where Jesus and Mary, surrounded by choirs of angels, await him to give him joy for all eternity!

Happy is the traveler who does not seek for a dwelling place here, but who always aspires to reign and to live with Christ in heaven!

Happy are the poor and indigent who each day come to ask for bread at the table of the Master, and who do not cease to plead, praying until they have received a few crumbs!

Happy is he who is called to the feast of the Lamb, and approaches daily the banquet of the altar while waiting for the eternal banquet of heaven!

II.

Every time that the faithful receive Communion, or that the priest offers the Holy Sacrifice, so often do they receive in union with Jesus and Mary food for the soul.

He who communicates becomes by that act the apostle of Jesus, the page of Mary, the companion of the saints, the brother of the apostles, an intimate of God, the kinsman of the saints, and the heir of the happiness of heaven.

Flee confusion, avoid dissipation of the soul, watch carefully over both your heart and your senses, if you wish to please Jesus and Mary.

You will then receive all succor from on high, and, always, when you call for aid in the midst of perils, and in the greatest dangers, you will be heard by the Master Himself.

It is thus that once on a tempestuous night the frightened
apostles called upon Jesus. At once Jesus coming to them said,
"Why are you fearful? O men of little faith! I am here; do
not fear."

The voice of Jesus has the sweetness that consoles, the strength
that supports, the joy that reassures, the grace that absolves,
the goodness that pardons.

The voice of Mary also reconciles, and adds to the sweetness of
the honey the strength of its comb.

III. Prayer:

Oh, how pleasing, sweet and agreeable to hear your voice,
O Mary, my Mother!

What voice? The caressing and divine voice heard by John, the
beloved disciple, the voice that said, "My son, behold your
Mother."

The apostle heard it from the lips of Jesus. I wish to hear it
from your own lips.

O Mary! Say to your servant, "My son, here is your Mother:
here she is near to you."

At this voice, my soul, rekindled with joy, will find again
strength and consolation, as John found them on receiving
his Mother.

Let your voice, sweeter than all others, come to my ears! O Mary,
let it come to my heart! Your fruitful maternal words will
bring to me the gifts of the Holy Ghost.

(Monastic Enchiridion, Chap. V)

HOMILY

SPIRITUAL COMMUNION

I. Spiritual communion consists in the ardent desire to receive sacramental Communion. Mary, more than all other saints, can serve us as model and exemplar.

Even before she received the Divine Child in her womb, Mary aspired to communicate in thought with God. Through her love, she drew God to her, said St. Bernard.

II. Thus spiritual communion ought to be to every Christian. In Communion, it is the communicant who is transformed into that which he receives, and not the contrary, as in material manducation. When I receive Communion, said Rodin, I absorb a force which transforms me.

III. To attain this transformation, the soul requires recollection and devotion, that is to say, the complete oblation of the whole being to God. It is through Mary that this offering is the most pleasing to God. Let us go to Jesus through Mary.

MEDITATION

DEVOTION

Devotion, this is the offering made to God of what is best in the creature. Devotion cannot exist without the total oblation of the heart and the will.

Devotion is a mysterious and sublime act. It is a gift and an offering. It is also the portion of a woman and of a virgin, still more than that of a man of action. It is something sweet and ecstatic.

But it is an ecstasy to which every soul may attain by effort over himself. It is necessary to give, and to give oneself in order to devote oneself well: to devote oneself is truly to possess devotion.

Let us imitate Mary, and let us remember that Mary acted by virtues and not by words in her life.

Practice: Be recollected for a moment each evening before retiring.

Thought: O Mary, offer us to Jesus upon your arms, even as a mother offers her child to you.

CHAPTER XXVI

THE MATERNAL INTERCESSION OF MARY

I.

It is a salutary practice for all to evoke the memory of the holy and glorious Virgin Mary and to confide themselves to her in all dangers as an unhappy child confides himself to his mother.

The name of Mary frequently invoked brings to the soul assurance and comfort. In her turn, Mary is always ready to say to her Son the word of grace in favor of anyone who suffers and who bears the burden of sorrow.

Indeed, if Mary did not intercede in heaven for the world, how would the world be able to subsist in the midst of the sins, and in the mire of the vice in which it would dwell?

If it is a duty for all the faithful to invoke Mary, it is an obligation for Religious and for devout souls: they make a formal profession of virtue and they aspire to the perfection of heaven by forsaking the world and the things of the world.

But, first of all, what ought you to ask of Mary? In the first place, pardon for the sins committed; next, the grace of practicing humility, because it is humility alone which is pleasing to God.

You ought also to seek out poverty and not to glorify yourself for gifts received, if you do not wish to lose your poverty itself.

II.

Lament to be still so far from these qualities which alone may merit the name of virtues: sincere humility, total poverty, complete obedience, perfect charity.

94

All these qualities in their perfection are found blended in Mary.

Prostrate yourself therefore at her feet as one poor and a beggar, and come to ask for a small share at least of these beautiful virtues which alone can lead to a degree of perfection that you are unable to reach without them.

Seek all that you desire to obtain from God, through Mary, for her power extends over the earth and over purgatory.

Her glory is great and her grace is powerful, surpassing that of the archangels, the angels, and the saints, rising to God who is the cause of her grandeur and glory.

But this power, these glories and these favors, she has them that she may distribute them to us who live here below and who ask her for them.

Lovingly confide yourself as a son to the tenderness and affection of this Mother whose prayers are received by God.

Ask only what is pleasing to her Son and what is useful for your own salvation; she knows your needs better than you do.

To ask pardon for your sins and to remain humble is what pleases God and Mary most. Indeed it is because of her humility that Mary glorified herself before God, whereas she always kept silence about the other virtues and the other graces.

Humility everywhere; humility in everything.

III. Prayer:

Come, O my soul, come to embrace the one whom you love! Cover with kisses Mary, your Mother and the Mother of God. Kiss also her Son Jesus, the most beautiful of children among all the children of men.

You, O Mary, are accustomed to hearing the prayer of the poor and of orphans, and you never send away unconsoled those who persevere in coming to pray to you.

You, O Mary, are the Virgin Mother of a God, you are the mysterious and loving tree, engendered by the eternal line of kings, the tree which has produced the mysterious flower announced for the salvation of the whole world.

Jesus, our Savior and the Savior of all, to whom be honor and glory for eternity!

(Cloister Discipline, Chap. XIV)

HOMILY

THE PROTECTION OF MARY AND OBJECTS OF PIETY

I.   The maternal intercession of Mary has a name more familiar to the heart, it is that of protectress. To protect is to intercede and also to intervene and to direct. This is certainly the role of Mary in relation to the faithful.

But again, we must ask for this protection. Besides, often, we have impulses rather than energetic desires in the spiritual life. To desire supposes an effort and effort belongs only to courage.

II.   To receive the protection of Mary, we must merit it. The petition and the effort are already a motive for obtaining it. To desire confidently, to act, to renew our resolutions, to multiply our acts of the will, here are the means of obtaining this protection.

III.   Far from that is the blind and slightly superstitious confidence sometimes attached to objects of piety themselves. Those are only signs and not generators of piety. Devotion ought to be enlightened, active, and rising above the aims of the earth.

MEDITATION

CONFIDENCE AND SUPERSTITION

Confidence is a virtue which supposes faith and reason. The word itself indicates this. We trust or we confide ourselves to someone whom we believe to be superior to ourselves, and it is reason which guides. Reason is attracted by grace in christian confidence. In superstition, on the contrary, we confide ourselves to blind forces, imaginary and non-existent. Reason is led astray and the soul is blinded. The will becomes inactive and the character or energy is exhausted little by little.

Superstition has degrees. We must avoid even the appearances which are often presented under the aspect of vain observances. Devotion to Mary is sometimes badly understood in this sense. This is no longer devotion, it is foolishness.

To confide oneself, to devote oneself, to perfect oneself, to rise, here is the devotion which pleases our Mother.

Practice: To examine yourself each evening in order to know what personal effort you have made during the day.

Thought: He who confides himself to Mary will be saved, said St. Ephrem.

CHAPTER XXVII

FREQUENT INVOCATION OF MARY

I.

Like to the fragrant myrrh, I give and I have given the sweetness of perfumes.

Reflect, O my son, reflect carefully on the example and the actions of Mary.

She is that myrrh, fragrant and choice which produced a perfume and a fruit, Jesus.

She is the one who carries to earth and to men the abundance of sweet consolations.

Guard in the depth of your heart the name of Mary and you will be consoled.

To be loved by Mary is to possess a treasure.

The love of Mary extinguishes the fire of the passions and brings to the soul the freshness of the virtues.

The love of Mary teaches you to scorn the world and to serve God in humility.

The love of Mary ever leads you away from evil and ever guides you to practice good.

II.

Therefore love Mary with a special love, and you will receive from her special graces.

Invoke Mary, and you will be victorious.

Honor Mary, and you will have happiness.

Two particular graces are the fruit of devotion to the Virgin Mary.

The first is to know how to praise God in prosperity; the second is to be able to be patient in adversity.

It is thus that Mary always glorified the Lord for the generous benefits she received from His hand while on earth.

It is thus that she showed herself in trials, always sweet and always ready to choose abasement rather than exaltation.

III. Prayer:

O Virgin most holy, O glorious Mary, O Mother, you are the gate of paradise, the source of life, the temple of the Lord, the beloved sanctuary of the Holy Ghost.

Whatever I can see of grace and beauty in human creatures; whatever I find of the sublime and great in the saints united to God in heaven: all this can I apply without error to your excellence and to your dignity.

It is very just and suitable that I apply myself, and with me all creatures, to praise unceasingly her whom I have chosen for advocate and mother, not only here below but in heaven beyond life, so as to merit through her eternal glory. The glory of Jesus, Her Son, thrice holy!

(Sermons to the Novices, XXV)

HOMILY

VOCAL PRAYER AND INVOCATIONS

I. Each thought is a real thing, a force. This force acts on the body itself. Be in your thought strong and active; your body will never be feeble.

This latent power which is in us is vivified by prayer and is heightened by its strength.

When this interior prayer is put into words, it acquires a double power. Herein lies the virtue of vocal prayer.

II. But this ought to be a prayer and not a recitation. True vocal prayer is that which is dictated by the heart and by inspiration. However, everyone not being poet or orator, we have recourse to the prayer of the Liturgy and of the Church, inspired by the Saints.

III. Such are true prayers and veritable invocations agreeable to God. The Office of the Blessed Virgin is, with the Rosary, the great vocal prayer and invocation which every devout soul should repeat often. Let us love liturgical prayers.

MEDITATION

Ejaculatory prayers are brief aspirations which we shoot as arrows into the sky, said St. Francis of Sales. They are outbursts and flashes of lightning. They bear the soul on high, and they win others.

Now, to bring to others a hope, a comfort, constitutes an act of heroic virtue, a work of mercy which brings us close to God. On the contrary, to discourage or to recriminate is to work against oneself and to pierce oneself with the arrows destined to be shot into the sky.

Invocations to Mary, the litanies of the Virgin, are the true ejaculatory prayers which we should have constantly on our lips.

Let us remember these when we feel depressed or only tempted.

Practice: Accustom yourself to say with feeling: Ave Maria!

Thought: We cry unto you, O Mary! *Ad te clamamus, O Maria.*

CHAPTER XXVIII

THE MEDIATION OF MARY WITH GOD

I.

The Disciple:
Grace flows from your lips, O Mary! Ah, yes, my queen and my
mother, speak, speak to my soul, you who are so gentle and so
compassionate to poor sinners.

Mary:
Yes, my son, I am the Mother of mercy to the heart filled with
compassion:
    I am the mysterious ladder of sinners,
    I am the hope and pardon of the culpable,
    I am the consolation of afflicted souls,
    I am the joy and the fruition of the blessed.
Come to me, all you who love me, come and you will be filled
with my consolations.
Come, because I have pity on all those who pray to me: Come
to me! Come everyone, just and sinners. I shall also pray to
the Eternal Son, my Son, so that He will pardon each of you
through the Holy Spirit.
I call to all of you, and I await all of you; I desire to see you all,
everyone of you, come to me. I scorn no sinner, indeed far
from that, I rejoice with the angels in heaven over one sinner
who is converted and returns.
Thus bears fruit the blood of my sweet Son, offered to God for
the salvation of the entire world.

Come to me, come children of men, my mother's heart protects
you with God.
I shall myself bear His aroused anger, if it be necessary, and I
shall appease Him until you are pardoned.
Change your ways and turn to God!
You have offended His love and His grace, but ask pardon and I
shall obtain for you indulgence and peace. I have been chosen
by God Himself to be mediatrix for you, between heaven and
you, between the world and God.

II. The Disciple:

O word filled with grace and sweetness! O kind word heard from heaven itself, word that consoles, word that comforts; word that delights the sinner and the just, voice of a mother, voice that resounds in the heart as a gentle harmony in heaven.

How is it that this honor comes to me today, that the Mother of my Savior deigns to speak to me? Yes, you are blessed, O my Mother, and your voice is a blessing!

You have milk and honey in your voice; the perfume of your words surpasses in sweetness all the perfumes of the universe.

My soul is transported at the sound of your voice, O Mary, and as soon as your gentle speech is heard my heart trembles and my whole being exults joyously, because you bring happiness to me.

I was sad and your voice reassures me, a voice so gentle that it seems to come from heaven.

I was sad and crushed in desolation, and you lift me up and comfort me.

You extend your hands to me, you touch me, and I am cured of my infirmity.

I could scarcely speak, and now I feel myself completely restored, induced to speak again and to proclaim your praises.

Life was a burden to me, and now death itself no longer makes me fearful, because I know that you are my advocate with God.

I confide myself and my cause to your tenderness, O Mother, now, in the future, and at every moment.

From the day you spoke to me, an orphan, I have been transformed into a new man, and I have felt in my soul new strength.

I was weighted down, without hope or life: at your call, O my Mother, I felt that a new courage, and a new joy were coming to lift me up.

III. Mary:

What is the matter, my child? Where are your enemies?

Go, fear nothing, I shall watch over you. I give to you assurance through my Son Jesus, your Brother, who made Himself your pontiff, your victim, and your intercessor.

Confide yourself to Him and be without fear, because if He is seated at the right of the Father as a judge, He is at the same time the master of death and the author of life.

From all eternity begotten by the Father, He was incarnate in time in my womb, so as to come and bring Redemption to the world.

He is, therefore, the unique source of all hope, the cause of all consolation, the foundation of all victory.

Let Jesus and Mary be always present in your memory, O my son, and you will never fear the blows of the enemy.

(Soliloquy of the Soul, Chap. XXIV)

HOMILY

THE ROLE OF MARY IN THE CHURCH

I. We often repeat that Mary is the mediatrix between God and men, without considering well this role of mediatrix. The mediation of Mary is only an intervention, whereas that of Jesus is an immolation. Mary is an advocate who intercedes; Jesus is the mediator who pays.

II. But the intervention of Mary, even as advocate, is a force; a power for us, because she excels in lifting us. Our soul, thus confident, acts on our own body and exalts it. The habit of effort maintains the vigor of faith and the force of love.

III. The role of Mary in the Church is a role of inspirer of beauty, generator of charm, and creator of poetry. These words say more in the spiritual life than they signify in real life. Religions in which the cult of the Virgin does not flourish are cold religions, stripped of grace. Thus Mary is called by the Church: *Causa nostrae laetitiae:* cause of our joy.

MEDITATION

THE MERCY OF MARY

Misericordiarum Mater: the mother of mercies, such is the title which the Liturgy gives to Mary. We understand, here, by mercy, the maternal compassion or the maternal intervention of Mary in favor of men.

True mercy belongs to God alone. Only He has the right of grace and of pardon, He loves to exercise it through His Mother. The gift thus assumes more sweetness and charm.

Mary has herself received from God all the mercies, that is to say, all the graces that a creature can receive: graces of body, graces of heart, graces of soul.

O Mary, be to us a tender Mother, a sweet Mother, a Mother all merciful!

Practice: To be compassionate to all the unfortunate and often to give them alms.

Thought: Mother of mercy, pray for us! *Mater misericordiae, ora pro nobis.*

CHAPTER XXIX

THE DIVINE INTERVENTION OF MARY

I. The Disciple:

Happy moment when you deign, O Mary, to visit my poor saddened soul!

Do not make me wait too long for this visit, O Mother, let me hear your words of consolation.

Your words exalt me and inflame me: they warm my heart and enlighten my mind.

Happy Mother, O Mary, who alone can at all times, give to us your children the milk of consolation, as once you gave the milk of your breast to Jesus, your Son.

You do not refuse compassionate aid to the one who asks you: even more, you grant your help to those who may offend you.

O Mother of tenderness and Mother of sweetness, Mother of mercy and Mother of love! incomparable Virgin, worthy to be loved, Mother who alone merited to have as Son, the Son of God Himself, born of you!

You are at the same time Mother to all and a Mother to each one of us. You give to all and to each his part of your heart and his portion of your love.

O Virgin blessed among all virgins, Mother of Men and Queen of Angels, come, snatch from me the weight of my sins, draw me far from earth and close to you!

Infuse into my softened soul your grace, like to the life-giving dew of the sky, so that from here on earth, I may feel that you are the Mother of mercy.

II. Mary:

I am, O my son, the Mother of beautiful love, of sweet fears and of tender words, I am the Mother of true consolations.

Exult in your heart on hearing my name, bow your head and greet me: you honor the Son in honoring the Mother.

I am, my child, the Mother of Jesus, and this title is my glory for eternity.

Reflect upon what Jesus is. He is the Son of God, the Savior of all, the King of heaven and earth,

He is the hope of the just and the peace of the meek. He is the strength of the weak and the way of the wanderers.

He is the support of those whom misfortune oppresses: He is the succor of those who suffer tribulation: He is the refuge of those who are of good heart.

My child, honor both the Son and the Mother, and you will be in return blessed by the Father.

You give honor and glory to Jesus each time that you honor me.

Place me as a seal upon your heart and as a seal upon your acts.

In all your works and in all your pleasures, in the midst of your joys and sadnesses, let the name of Jesus and the name of Mary be often on your lips and always in your heart.

III. The Disciple:

Let all peoples and tongues, let all creatures serve you, O Mary! Let all bow before you! Let the heavens say of you: Rejoice, O Mary, throughout eternity; and let the earth respond: Rejoice for eternity and beyond.

Let all the saints proclaim your name, O Mother, your sublime name, and let all the blessed rejoice before you and before your Son, Our Lord and our eternal Master.

(Soliloquy of the Soul, Chap. XXV)

HOMILY

The Force and Powers of Mary

I.   Force and power are prerogatives of sovereignty. But these prerogatives can never be exercised. They are for sovereigns of a hard heart and a distracted soul.

Mary is a sovereign, but also a mother. If it is so pleasing and so beautiful to see in history, queens uniting to the prestige of royalty the privilege of beauty and the charm of tenderness, what can we imagine of Mary?

II.   Dominion belongs to her, as co-redemptrix of the human race, thus the Liturgy proclaims it: *exaudietur pro sua reverentia.* The exercise of this force is facilitated for her by her tenderness in regard to those who are her children, adopted in the person of St. John at Calvary.

III.   The powers of Mary extend to spiritual favors, but pour forth sometimes even in corporal graces. Both are granted only to pure hearts and to souls disposed to active strivings toward heaven. The Assumption of Mary ought to be the model of our ascension toward God.

MEDITATION

Intercession of Mary

To intercede is to intervene with supplication in favor of someone, but also with the certain hope of obtaining the petition. Mary, by her title of Queen of Heaven and Mother of Men, intervenes in our favor when we ask her for her intercession.

In the beautiful Liturgical Office of the Virgin, inspired by Scripture, we say at each Psalm: *O Maria, intercede pro nobis, ad Dominum Deum nostrum.* O Mary intercede for us with Him who is your Lord and your Son, but who is our God.

We speak to God as to a Sovereign and to a Judge; but you, you speak to Him as to a Son and a Protector. We also have recourse to your intercession, O Mary, O our Mother!

Practice: A holy and salutary habit consists in carrying a rosary or wearing a medal.

Thought: Let us go to Jesus through Mary: *Ad Jesum per Mariam.*

CHAPTER XXX

OF THE ETERNAL ROYALTY OF LOVE

I.

Upon her head, like that of a queen, is placed a crown of twelve stars. These twelve stars on the brow of Mary are the twelve prerogatives of the Queen and of the Mother before God in heaven.

She possesses, indeed, in the Church Triumphant, surpassing all other blessed spirits, four special prerogatives:

the power of listening with great goodness,

of condescending with great mercy,

of intervening for us with great power,

and of succoring on earth with great ease.

She, has besides, in the Church Triumphant, four privileges, outstanding among all:

she is resplendent more than all others;

she is glorified more than all others;

she is loved more tenderly than all others;

she is honored more fervently than all others.

Mary possesses also, in relation to the Trinity, four particular favors, which are for her like brilliant stars midst fainter stars.

Better, truly, than those who contemplate the glory of the Divine Trinity,

she contemplates fully the Divine Trinity Itself:

she knows with greater joy its sweetness,

she comprehends with greater profundity its mysteries,

she tastes with greater charm its richness.

II.

Listen again, listen devoutly, to what the greatest of the servants of Mary, the doctor of gentle speech, St. Bernard, said to his Religious about the stars which form a crown on the forehead of the Virgin:

No one can estimate the importance of the jewels, no one can count the number of the gems which adorn the diadem of Mary in Heaven.

It is an undertaking above our power, that of examining the value, or of scrutinizing the composition of her brilliant aureole. We shall undertake to do so with humility.

Without wishing to penetrate the secrets of the Lord, it seems that one can see in the twelve stars the twelve prerogatives of our Mother.

We find indeed in the Virgin Mary,
>   privileges granted to her soul,
>   privileges infused into her heart,
>   privileges attached to her body.

And if we multiply this number three,
>   by the number of the four known favors,
>   we shall find the number of twelve stars
>   which shine on the brow of Mary, our Queen.

We find these wonders,
>   at her birth,
>   in the salutation she received from the angel,
>   in the overshadowing of her by the Holy Spirit,
>   and finally in the conception of Jesus Himself.

The holy doctor goes on to enumerate the circumstances of the life of our Mother in which grace brought its favors.

III.

Let us meditate therefore, often and with piety, on the life and deeds of Mary. Let us chant hymns and canticles in her honor, on the days of her solemnities.

Come before her altar and before her image, incline your head, kneel before her, as if you were seeing Mary herself present before you.

Raise your eyes and contemplate Mary speaking with the angels, or better still, Mary holding on her knees her son Jesus:

In contemplating the Mother of Mercy, say then, with a burst of confident love:

IV. Prayer:

O most loving Virgin Mary, Mother of God, Queen of Heaven, Mistress of the Earth,

O you, the Joy of Saints, and the Salvation of sinners, listen to the appeals of our repentant hearts! Listen to the desires of our souls at prayer!

Come to the help of the poor and the infirm! Renew the courage of the afflicted! Protect your children against their enemies!

Deliver them from the snares of the devils. Lead them near to you in blessedness in heaven, where you reign with your Son in the midst of the elect for all eternity!

(Cloistral Discipline, Chap. XIV)

HOMILY

ROYALTY OF HEART

I.   Everything is sold or bought on the earth: power, favor, gold, conscience itself. Only the heart is not sold; it gives itself or does not give itself, fashioned as it is with a spark of royalty.

A great orator has said: the heart is the whole of man, it is the raison d'être of a woman. The heart of Mary is the greatest of hearts, after the Heart of Jesus. Was not the Heart of Jesus fashioned from a bit of the human heart of Mary?

II.   The Heart of Jesus, united to the divinity in the person of Christ, has transmitted by its contact with the heart of His Mother something of Its grandeur and beauty to the heart of Mary. Mary is therefore queen by her heart, as she is queen by her human destiny. Her heart vibrates with more force than the heart of any other creature. It is less sublime than the Heart of God, but it is unique in heaven and earth.

III.   Oh! how sweet it is to feel yourself near this heart which has loved with a mother's love an Infant God, and which loves with the same maternal love all the children of men.

MEDITATION

THE PERPETUITY OF LOVE

Love is not a simple sentiment; it is a gigantic force: women hold a power which they do not know. Only Mary has known what power the heart of a mother has. To know how to love, and to love always, is an ardent life, an active life, a very short life. Not to love is to be dead.

Love addresses itself to the spirited person who vibrates and not to the lifeless or inactive person. Love supposes beauty, and sometimes creates it or exalts it.

Let us love Mary! She has beauty, she has grace, she has charm. No creature equals her; no woman surpasses her. She comes next after God, as Dante sings.

Let us say to her then with the heavenly poet: O Mother, O Queen, O Mary, help us to love you, help us to praise you.

You are beauty, *la beltà,* and we cannot admire you enough.
You are goodness, *la bontà,* and we cannot praise you enough.

We say to you therefore the only word worthy of you, the word sent from heaven, the word of the Archangel: Ave Maria!

Practice: Imitate the early Christians and often recite the Liturgical Office of the Holy Virgin.

Thought: O Mary, bless us and our families.
Nos cum prole pia, benedicat Virgo Maria.